SKILL SHARPENERS
Grammar & 6 Punctuation

Writing: Bryan Langdo
Editing: Teera Safi
Lisa Vitarisi Mathews
Copy Editing: Kathleen Jorgensen
Art Direction: Yuki Meyer
Illustration: Bryan Langdo
Design/Production: Yuki Meyer
Jessica Onken

EMC 9956

Evan-Moor®
Helping Children Learn

Visit
teaching-standards.com
to view a correlation
of this book.
This is a free service.

**Correlated to
Current Standards**

**Congratulations on your purchase of some of the
finest teaching materials in the world.**

EVAN-MOOR CORP.
phone 1-800-777-4362, fax 1-800-777-4332.
Entire contents © 2019 EVAN-MOOR CORP.
18 Lower Ragsdale Drive, Monterey, CA 93940-5746. Printed in China.

CPSIA: Asia Pacific Offset Ltd, Kowloon, Hong Kong [10/2020]

Contents

Concepts:
A noun phrase is a word or group of words that contains a noun or pronoun and all the words, phrases, or clauses that modify it;

A comma is used to separate the day from the year in a date and the year from the rest of a sentence

Read the story.

Grandpa's Trip Around the World

Grandpa has taken many vacations to exotic places. Now he's planning his biggest trip ever: a voyage around the world! He and I have been reading about other people who have done this. On August 10, 1519, a group of men set sail with a fleet of ships from Spain. They returned three years later, on September 8, 1522. That was the first time in history anyone had completely circumnavigated the globe. Grandpa will board a plane in New York on November 30, 2019, and head first to Europe. He'll visit friends in London and Paris before taking a cruise around the Greek islands. He needs to be in India by January 9, 2020, because he has a ticket for a train ride. After that, Grandpa will travel to many places throughout Asia and fly home from China on March 12, 2020. I told Grandpa that I wished I could go, too. He smiled and said he'd plan another, even bigger, trip for us to go on someday.

Read the rules. Answer the questions.

FIND IT!

Grammar A noun phrase is a word or group of words that contains a noun or pronoun and all the words, phrases, or clauses that modify it. A noun phrase functions as a noun, and it can contain one word or more than one word.

How many green noun phrases can you find in the story? _____

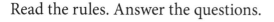

Punctuation We write a comma ⟨,⟩ to separate the day and year in a date and to set off the year from the rest of the sentence.

How many orange commas can you find in the story? _____

Noun Phrases

Skills:

Identify noun phrases;

Produce a sentence that has a noun phrase

A **noun phrase** is a phrase that contains a noun or pronoun and all the words, phrases, or clauses that help describe it. A noun phrase can be one word or more than one word. The articles **a**, **an**, and **the** are part of the noun phrase.

These are noun phrases:

the gigantic airplane	**many of the people in Alaska**
trains	**his black cat sitting on the fence**
some ships in the harbor	**my aunt who went to Thailand**

A noun phrase functions as a noun in a sentence. A sentence may have one noun phrase or more than one.

> **Whitney and Peter** chose **a postcard** and mailed it to **their aunt in Paris.**

Read the sentence. Then underline all of the noun phrases in the sentence.

1. My family travels a lot.

2. Kwon went on a cruise around some islands.

3. The jet flies over the mountains in Colorado.

4. The train's restaurant car served food that I like.

5. While his parents relaxed on the deck of the ship, Ethan rode the water slide.

6. Kids my age were also on the Alaskan cruise.

7. Anisa got the seat next to the window on her flight to London.

8. Mom was able to rent a car at the airport in Denver.

Write a sentence that has a noun phrase. Circle the noun phrase in your sentence.

9. _____

_____

Skill Sharpeners: Grammar and Punctuation • EMC 9956 • © Evan-Moor Corp.

Travel

The Mysterious Passenger

Write noun phrases from the word box or some of your own noun phrases to complete the the story. You can make the story serious or silly. You can use pronouns and single words, too.

a cross-country trip	the mysterious figure	a train
a fierce, dreadful storm	many other people	he
a paperback novel	a mustache that curls	an eye patch
a man with a scowl	the scary character	books to read
the dark-clothed man	the odd traveler	a black cape

Last summer, my entire family went on _____.

We rode on _____. There were _____ riding,

too. I had brought my phone and _____ on the trip. On a very

dark night, the second night of our travels, there was _____.

I was alternating between looking out the window and reading my spooky

_____. Suddenly, out of the corner of my eye, I saw

_____ in a nearby seat. When I looked out the window

again, I could see the reflection of _____ in the window,

and _____ was looking right at me! I wanted to get a good

picture of what _____ looked like, so I observed the reflection

closely. I saw that _____ had _____ and

_____, just like the disguise the half-monster man used in

my book! Just then, _____ arose from the seat. I'll never know

what _____ was going to do, though, because Mom came

and took me to _____ at that moment.

Travel

Commas with Dates

Write a **comma** between the day and the year in a date.

    July 8**,** 2022

Write a comma after the year in a date to set it off
from the rest of the sentence.

    We'll set out on March 14**,** 2021**,** for our cross-country trip.

Read the sentence. Then write a comma or commas where they belong.

1. The last time I took a flight was on April 4 2018.

2. The next cruise leaves on May 12 2022 and goes
   up through Scandinavia.

3. The world's first commercial flight occurred on January 1 1914.

4. Mom hasn't had to travel for work since September 29 2018.

5. We picked up the rental car on November 18 2018 and
   arrived on Thanksgiving.

6. August 4 2017 was a special day for me because
   that's when we arrived in Hawaii.

7. I boarded the cruise ship on June 13 2018 and sailed across
   the Atlantic.

8. Our train will depart on October 12 2021 from Flagstaff, Arizona.

9. We should arrive in Stockholm on February 15 2022.

10. Unfortunately, our flight for May 9 2023 is cancelled.

11. Our cruise goes from October 28 2024 to November 6 2024.

12. March 11 2021 will be the first day of our trip.

13. On April 19 2018 we saw three whales alongside
    our ship.

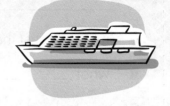

Skill Sharpeners: Grammar and Punctuation • EMC 9956 • © Evan-Moor Corp.

Postcards from Our Journey

Skills:
Use visual information;
Expand noun phrases

There are so many interesting things to see when you travel around the world! Look at each photo, and read the noun below it. Then write words before or after the noun to make it a longer noun phrase. The first one has been done for you.

1

the landscape <u>covered in snow and frosted trees</u>

2

_____

_____

_____ Australian Outback

3

a bird _____

_____

_____

4

a volcano _____

_____

_____

Travel

Write It Right!

The sentences below have misplaced noun phrases and punctuation errors in dates. Read the sentences carefully. Then rewrite them correctly.

Skills:

Identify misplaced noun phrases in sentences;

Identify missing punctuation with dates;

Write sentences with correctly placed noun phrases;

Write sentences correctly using commas with dates

1. Left the station in Chicago our train on February 9 2016.

_____

_____

2. On June 8 2022 departs from the airport in Newark our flight.

_____

_____

3. The Caribbean cruise went from December 20 2017 until January 7 2018.

_____

_____

4. On May 26 2023 we will start our road trip by heading west.

_____

_____

5. It's been a tradition in our family since April 9 2013 Hawaii to visit each year.

_____

_____

6. From October 19 2022 until January 2 2023 we will be in Europe.

_____

_____

Travel

Skill Sharpeners: Grammar and Punctuation • EMC 9956 • © Evan-Moor Corp.

Come Fly Away!

Read the sentences below. Then write commas in the dates where they belong.

1. There's a flight to Denver on July 5 2021.

2. We fly from Rio de Janeiro to Lima on August 12 2023.

3. We'll see you on October 10 2020!

4. The plane lands on January 15 2022.

5. January 18 2024 is perfect for me.

6. Is March 25 2021 okay?

7. November 20 2022 is when we'll get together.

8. We're set to leave on May 21 2024!

9. I think February 9 2023 is when we'll take our flight.

10. Can you make it on August 6 2024?

11. I'll arrive on March 14 2021.

12. If September 8 2022 doesn't work, we'll find another date.

13. We land on May 7 2022 so we'll see you then.

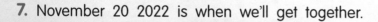

Look at the number that comes before each comma that you wrote. If it is a sentence in which you wrote two commas, look at only the number that comes before the first comma you wrote. Find the matching letter in the box below, and write it on the correct line or lines to discover the hidden message.

1-A	2-B	3-C	4-D	5-E	6-F	7-G	8-H	9-I
10-J	11-K	12-L	13-M	14-N	15-O	16-P	17-Q	18-R
19-S	20-T	21-U	22-V	23-W	24-X	25-Y	26-Z	

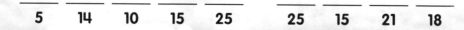

__ __ __ __ __   __ __ __ __
5 14 10 15 25   25 15 21 18

__ __ __ __ __ __
6 12 9 7 8 20

Travel

River Cruise

Write a sentence to explain what a noun phrase is.

1. _____

_____

Circle the items that are noun phrases.

2. his flight to Japan   3. airport   4. find your luggage

5. all the suitcases   6. observe   7. the food tray that is in front of me

Read the paragraph. Write commas with dates where they belong, and underline all the noun phrases. Remember that a noun phrase includes all the words that describe the noun or pronoun.
HINT Dates are nouns.

8.   Dylan's mom was looking at a brochure that had arrived in the mail. It advertised cruises in different parts of the world. "A river cruise!" exclaimed Mom. "It stops in various cities throughout Europe. It departs on July 30 2023."

    "That is near my birthday!" said Dylan. He was born on July 28 2012 and was glad to have a summer birthday. Suddenly, Mom remembered July was not going to work. They are going to their family reunion in Maine then. Another cruise was available on February 14 2024 though. "Sweet!" Dylan shouted.

Write a sentence that has a noun phrase. Circle the noun phrase or phrases in your sentence.

9. _____

_____

Travel

Concepts:
A verb phrase is a word or group of words that contains a verb and includes all the words that relate to the action, including modifiers and objects;

Commas are used to set off nonessential appositives in sentences

Read the story.

Green Horizon

I visited Paul, my brother, this past weekend. He graduates from art school soon. I saw his art exhibit in the school's gallery, and it looked incredible. His art, photography, reminds me of the work of my favorite photographer, Diane Arbus. I recognized one big photograph from winter break the last time I visited. It is my favorite of Paul's photographs. Most of the image is yellow, but a large streak of green cuts across the middle.

"I named it 'Green Horizon,'" Paul said.

We stayed at the gallery for a while, and I met some of his friends.

After we left the gallery, Paul and I ate lunch, veggie burgers, and then we took our cameras to a park. For the next hour or so, we took pictures of the people we saw passing by.

Before I came home, Paul had a surprise for me. He wanted to sell most of his pictures but gave "Green Horizon," the one I loved, to me!

Read the rules. Answer the questions.

Grammar   A verb phrase is a word or group of words that contains a verb and includes all the words that relate to the action. A verb phrase can include objects, or the nouns that receive the action. The phrase may contain one word or more than one.

FIND IT!

How many green verb phrases can you find in the story? _____

Punctuation   We write a comma (,) or commas to set off an appositive that is not essential in the sentence. An appositive is a noun phrase that renames a noun and gives more detail about it.

How many orange commas can you find in the story? _____

Verb Phrases

A **verb phrase** is a phrase that contains a verb and any objects, prepositions, adverbs, helping verbs, and other words that relate to the action. A verb phrase can be one word or more than one word. These are verb phrases:

paints   **looks at a painting**   **sculpts with clay**

In a sentence, the complete predicate is a verb phrase.

Visitors to The Art Institute **can see art from different periods in history.**

Read the sentence. Then underline the verb phrase.

1. Miss Marguerite's art class visits an art museum.

2. Maisie and Darnell worked on a mural at school.

3. I squeeze the paint tube.

4. The students love using clay.

5. The clay feels nice.

6. The teacher places the pottery in the kiln.

7. Let's hang these drawings on the wall.

8. The portrait captures Divya's personality perfectly.

9. Mason reads a book about Picasso.

10. Jaedyn finishes her drawing after school.

Write a sentence that has a verb phrase. Then circle the entire verb phrase.

11. _____

_____

Still Life

Skills:
Identify verb phrases;

Produce a sentence with a verb phrase;

Produce a sentence with a linking verb;

Distinguish between action and linking verbs

A verb phrase may use an **action verb** or a **linking verb**. Read the sentence, and underline the verb phrase. Then write *action* or *linking* to describe the verb in the phrase.

1. Mr. Gilberto places items on a table. _____

2. The items look interesting. _____

3. Zeke paints slowly. _____

4. Roxy creates a glass bottle with the paint. _____

5. Mohammad washes his paintbrush. _____

6. Dylan is talented. _____

7. The students make nice drawings. _____

8. Some objects are difficult to paint. _____

9. Nathan's paintbrush glides across the canvas. _____

10. Zoe becomes quiet. _____

11. She concentrates on her painting. _____

12. Mr. Gilberto advises Fritz. _____

13. The teacher seems happy with the students' work. _____

14. Sam is done with her painting. _____

15. Everyone admires one another's amazing work. _____

Write a sentence with a verb phrase that uses a linking verb.

16. _____

_____

Commas with Appositives

We write a **comma** or **commas** to set off a **nonessential appositive**. An appositive is a noun phrase that renames a noun and gives more detail about it. When an appositive is nonessential, it is not needed to understand who or what the sentence is about.

My mom, <u>the artist in our family</u>, makes statues in our garage.

appositive

When an appositive is **essential**, it is part of the original noun and is needed to understand who or what the sentence is about. We do not use a comma with an essential appositive.

My mom <u>the sculptor</u> acts very differently

from my mom <u>the family member</u>.

Read the sentence. Underline the original noun, and circle the appositive.

1. Albert drew a peregrine falcon, his favorite bird.

2. Miss Han, our art teacher, designs jewelry.

Read the sentence. Then write a comma or commas to separate the appositive from the rest of the sentence.

3. Gabrielle drew a picture of Nugget her kitten.

4. We ran out of two paint colors red and green.

5. We had a guest speaker Ms. Croy in our class today.

Read the sentence. Look at the punctuation. Then circle the appositive, and write *essential* or *nonessential* to describe it.

6. Today we met Al Ziegfeld, a famous artist. _____

7. Our neighbor Charles owns an art gallery. _____

Photographs Tell a Story

Skills:
Use visual information;

Produce a verb phrase;

Draw to show understanding of a verb phrase

Look at the photograph, and read the subject of the sentence. Then complete the sentence by writing a verb phrase about what you see in the photograph.

1

The girl _____

_____ .

2

This family _____

_____ .

3

An elephant _____

_____ .

4

These boys _____

_____ .

Read the verb phrase below.
Draw a picture of a subject doing what the verb phrase describes.

paints a family portrait

Skills:

Identify comma errors with appositives;

Identify misplaced verb phrases;

Write sentences correctly using commas with appositives;

Write sentences with correctly placed verb phrases

Write It Right!

The sentences below have misplaced verb phrases and comma errors with appositives. Some sentences have missing or misplaced commas or commas that are not needed. Read the sentences carefully. Then write them correctly.

1. Ava my friend is a very talented artist.

_____

_____

2. My, Aunt, Kemala a sculpting demonstration did for my class.

_____

_____

3. Fills an entire wall our class mural the one with the rainforest.

_____

_____

4. Painted a picture of me and all my other brothers my brother Marco.

_____

_____

5. Looks better than my red, painting my latest painting the blue one.

_____

_____

6. Mr. Vernassi my art teacher says art can be healing.

_____

_____

Skill Sharpeners: Grammar and Punctuation • EMC 9956 • © Evan-Moor Corp.

Art

Appositive Bingo!

Read the sentences on the bingo card. Color the squares that have sentences with correct punctuation.

Skills:
Identify sentences with correct punctuation to set off nonessential appositives;

Write commas to set off nonessential appositives

BINGO

Jamal visited the Whitney, an art museum.	Miss Emily a graphic designer talked to our art class.	Caleb my cousin is studying art in school.	I drew an animal a grizzly bear.	*Mona Lisa,* a painting by Leonardo DaVinci, is at the Louvre.
Dad and I spent yesterday Saturday drawing.	My grandma went to The Art Institute, an art school, to study.	Ms. Green my art teacher helps me.	Sanjay painted a picture, a flower, for his mom.	Tyler my little brother got into my art supplies again!
Dominique my best friend draws really well.	I'm giving this painting to Jessica my sister.	Can I borrow a marker, a red one?	Petros a kid in my class draws great superheroes.	My next-door neighbor Mr. DeMarco paints landscapes.
We learned about Rembrandt a painter.	Suki painted a portrait of Surfer, her dog.	I bought some art supplies paints and brushes.	Uncle Ryu, an illustrator, draws comic books.	Bernard the best artist in our class will be famous someday.
Aunt Roxy has a weekly art show in a coffee house, The Scalded Bean.	I got some advice from Miss Zoe my art teacher.	I painted a watercolor of Fiona my good friend.	Today we used clay my favorite material.	Mr. Hua, a guide at the art museum, is hilarious.

BONUS Now write commas where they belong on the squares you did not color on the bingo card.

ART

Skills:

Explain what a verb phrase is;

Explain what an appositive is;

Identify verb phrases;

Write commas to set off nonessential appositives;

Distinguish between essential and nonessential appositives

The Art Department

Explain what a verb phrase is.

1. _____

_____

Explain what an appositive is.

2. _____

_____

Read the sentence. Then circle the entire verb phrase.

3. Aunt Anita values all the art she has.

4. Mom and Dad hung a creepy portrait in the guest bedroom.

5. Grandma owns some beautiful pieces of art.

Read the sentence. Then write a comma or commas to set off the nonessential appositive.

6. Mom takes me to The Art Department an art supply store.

7. Dana the owner of the store shows me where the sketchbooks are.

8. I pick out a Zoomline my favorite type of pen.

9. I bump into Mr. Orlando my art teacher.

10. He's buying oil paint the kind of paint he always uses.

Read the sentence. Use the punctuation to figure out what type of appositive it contains. Then write *essential* or *nonessential* to describe it.

11. I found a book, a complete guide to sculpting. _____

12. The popular art store Paintfully Colorful is another store we shop at sometimes. _____

Skill Sharpeners: Grammar and Punctuation • EMC 9956 • © Evan-Moor Corp.

Concepts:
Proper adjectives are formed from proper nouns;

Commas are used to set off nonrestrictive elements in sentences

Read the text.

A Collection of City-States

Long before Greece was a country, it was a collection of city-states. **Greek** city-states, which had their own laws and armies, were quite distinct from one another. Sparta, which was ruled by warriors, had a fearsome army. **Spartan** boys, who began training at the age of seven, had to join the military. The city-state of Corinth invested in public works projects, which kept their citizens busy working. **Corinthian** citizens enjoyed luxuries such as bathhouses, or buildings with baths for the public. Argos, made up of multiple districts, was a long-time rival of Sparta. **Argive** citizens became renowned traders. Megara, located on the coast, granted its citizens a lot of freedom. **Megarian** sailors traveled extensively throughout the Mediterranean Sea. The greatest of the city-states was Athens, named for the goddess Athena. **Athenian** schools were considered the best of all the city-states' schools. Culture and the arts thrived in Athens. It was also the birthplace of democracy. As you can see, each city-state made a unique contribution to Greek civilization.

Read the rules. Answer the questions.

FIND IT!

Grammar **Proper adjectives**, such as the names of geographic places, are formed from proper nouns. Proper adjectives are capitalized.

How many purple **proper adjectives** can you find in the text? _____

- -

Punctuation We write a **comma** (,) or **commas** to set off nonrestrictive elements, or words, phrases, or clauses that give extra information that is not essential in a sentence.

How many orange **commas** can you find in the text? _____

Ancient Civilizations

Proper Adjectives

Proper adjectives are formed from proper nouns.
Proper adjectives describe nouns, as other adjectives do.
Proper adjectives are capitalized.

Proper Noun	Proper Adjective	Proper Noun	Proper Adjective
Australia	Australian	France	French
Greece	Greek	China	Chinese
Vietnam	Vietnamese	Ethiopia	Ethiopian
North America	North American	Hawaii	Hawaiian
Bolivia	Bolivian	Egypt	Egyptian

Read the proper noun. Then write the proper adjective for the proper noun.

1. Greece _____

2. Ethiopia _____

3. Hawaii _____

4. Boliva _____

5. North America _____

6. Egypt _____

7. Vietnam _____

8. France _____

9. Australia _____

10. China _____

Write a sentence using at least one proper adjective from the rule box.

11. _____

_____

Ancient Civilizations

Ancient Mesopotamia

Skills:

Identify proper adjectives;

Write proper adjectives;

Use proper adjectives;

Form proper adjectives

Ancient Mesopotamia is often called "The Cradle of Civilization" because it is the site of the oldest-known civilization. Read each sentence below. Then circle the proper adjective.

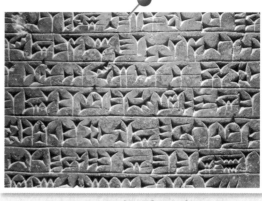

an example of ancient cuneiform writing

1. Mesopotamian engineers built canals.

2. Harranian residents lived in the ancient city of Harran in Mesopotamia.

3. King Hammurabi was a Babylonian king.

4. Assyrian traders traveled throughout Mesopotamia.

5. Cuneiform, a Sumerian method of writing, was developed around 3000 BCE.

6. Cuneiform was eventually replaced with the Phoenician alphabet.

7. Cyrus II, a Persian king, conquered Babylon in 539 BCE.

8. In the Greek language, Mesopotamia means "the land between two rivers."

9. The Iraqi city of Baghdad is located in what used to be Mesopotamia.

Write a proper adjective to complete the sentence.

10. A person from Egypt is _____.

11. People from Canada are _____.

12. A person from Japan is _____.

13. People from Mesopotamia were

_____.

14. A person from Africa is _____.

ruins of the ancient city of Harran in Mesopotamia

Ancient Civilizations

Punctuation Rule

Commas with Nonrestrictive Elements

statue of Emperor Augustus

We write a **comma** or **commas** to set off a nonrestrictive element in a sentence. A nonrestrictive element is a word, phrase, or clause that gives extra information about a subject in the sentence. If a nonrestrictive element were removed from the sentence, the sentence would still be complete and make sense.

nonrestrictive element

Archaeologists found one type of object, toys, in abundance when excavating the area where the Indus River valley civilization had been.

nonrestrictive element

The Saraswati River, which the Indus River valley civilization depended on, is believed to have dried up thousands of years ago.

Read the sentence. Is the nonrestrictive element punctuated correctly? Write *yes* or *no*.

1. Augustus, who was the son of Julius Caesar, was the first Roman emperor. _____

2. The Aztecs who settled in Mexico in the 1300s were originally nomadic. _____

3. Romans raced chariots in the Circus Maximus arena one of the largest sports arenas ever built. _____

4. King Tutankhamun an Egyptian pharaoh died at the age of 19. _____

Read the sentence. Then write a comma or commas to set off the nonrestrictive element.

5. The Nile delta which leads to the sea allowed Egyptians to trade with Europe.

6. Montezuma an Aztec leader expanded the empire.

Find the Way Home!

Look at the maze. For each pair of travelers, draw a line that leads to their homeland. Use a different color for each group. On the journey, make sure each group's line passes through three proper adjectives that apply to the group. Don't pass through any proper adjectives that do not apply!

Skill:
Match proper adjectives to proper nouns

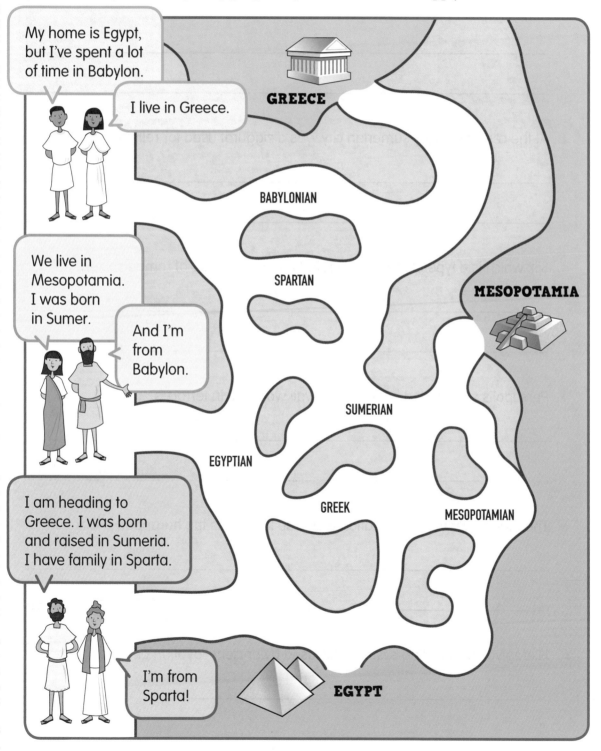

Ancient Civilizations

Write It Right!

a ziggurat

The sentences below have proper adjective errors and punctuation errors with nonrestrictive elements. Read the sentences carefully. Then write them correctly.

1. The Sphinx an ancient egyptian statue sits in Giza, Egypt.

_____

_____

2. At the center of every sumerian city was a ziggurat used for religious activities.

_____

_____

3. Silk which is a type of fabric fascinated many members of roman society.

_____

_____

4. Persepolis surrounded by a 30-foot wall was built in terraces.

_____

_____

5. The Indus River valley civilization was also known as the harappan civilization.

_____

_____

6. Hieroglyphics a writing system was used by ancient Egyptian people.

_____

_____

Skill Sharpeners: Grammar and Punctuation • EMC 9956 • © Evan-Moor Corp.

Sentence Spirals

Each spiral describes an ancient civilization. Read the sentences in each spiral, and write commas to set off the nonrestrictive elements. Then write the letter that comes directly after each comma you wrote in the spiral. After you write the letters, unscramble them to find out the name of the country where the ancient civilization was located. Write the country's name on the line.

Skills:
Write commas to set off nonrestrictive elements;

Unscramble letters to form words and solve a puzzle;

Use context to solve a puzzle

Ancient Civilizations

Spiral 1: People settled in this area having great networks of families and lineage. They grew rice a grain in abundance continuously for centuries. The land was ruled by dynasties and lineage. They grew rice a grain in abundance continuously for centuries.

Spiral 2: The people believed that pyramids enormous monuments built around crypts and tombs protected the bodies of pharaohs. Hieroglyphs their ancient writing symbols give us information young and inexperienced. Some pharaohs were teenagers young and inexperienced.

Spiral 3: The idea of democracy equal political rights for all emerged from this civilization. At first only certain people citizens who were male enjoyed these rights. Other advancements resulted from this culture. great scientific discoveries

_____

_____

_____

27

Ancient People

The Silk Road passed through mountains.

Explain what a proper adjective is.

1. _____

_____

Explain what a nonrestrictive element in a sentence is.

2. _____

_____

Write the proper adjective for the proper noun. Use a word from the box.

Persian	**Roman**	**Indian**	**Japanese**
Chinese	**Egyptian**	**Bolivian**	**Mexican**

3. Rome _____

4. China _____

5. India _____

6. Japan _____

Read the sentence. Then write *yes* or *no* to indicate whether
the capitalization in the sentence is correct.

7. The Silk Road was named for the Chinese silk that
was traded on that route. _____

8. The italian explorer Marco Polo traveled the Silk Road. _____

Read the sentence. Then write a comma or commas where they belong.

9. The Inca Empire a South American civilization performed skull surgeries.

10. The Incas used advanced farming techniques such as canals
and irrigation.

Ancient Civilizations

Concepts:

Intensive pronouns emphasize the subject;

Dashes and parentheses can be used instead of commas to set off nonrestrictive elements

Read the story.

Trouble Downtown!

Boom! A giant robot — made of steel—stomped through downtown. "Specter, what will we do?" Phantom asked.

"We will stop that robot **ourselves**," Specter said. "Then we'll find Doc Mezmer—the one who is surely controlling it."

"Right!" Phantom said. "Mezmer **himself** is the only villain capable of building such a machine." Vicki Vanish (a former employee of Doc's) told Phantom so **herself**.

The robot picked up a bus—filled with people—and shook it.

"I should help them," Phantom said. "Can you handle the Doc **yourself**?"

"No need." Specter pointed at the people—who were escaping the doomed bus. Once it was empty, the bus **itself** was crushed by the robot's enormous hand.

Specter's communicator device (which served as a direct line to the mayor) beeped. It was a message from the mayor **herself**. She sounded annoyed. "Are you two going to get rid of that robot, or do I need to do it **myself**?" she asked.

"Sorry, Mayor," Specter said. "We're on it!"

Read the rules. Answer the questions.

Grammar Intensive pronouns emphasize, or draw attention to, the subject of a sentence. These are intensive pronouns:

myself	yourself	himself	herself
itself	ourselves	yourselves	themselves

FIND IT!

How many blue **intensive pronouns** can you find in the story? _____

- -

Punctuation We write **dashes** (—) or **parentheses** (( )) to set off nonrestrictive elements. A nonrestrictive element gives extra information about a subject. We always use parentheses in pairs.

How many orange **dashes** and **pairs of parentheses** can you find in the story?

_____ dashes   _____ pairs of parentheses

Superheroes

Intensive Pronouns

An **intensive pronoun** emphasizes the subject of a sentence and draws more attention to the person or thing doing the action. These are intensive pronouns:

myself	yourself	himself	herself
itself	ourselves	yourselves	themselves

I **myself** am a highly respected superhero.

She can lift an entire school bus **herself**.

Note: Intensive pronouns are spelled the same as reflexive pronouns. But, unlike a reflexive pronoun, an intensive pronoun is not the object, or the receiver of the action, in a sentence.

Read the sentence. Then circle the intensive pronoun, and underline the subject that the intensive pronoun emphasizes.

1. I myself was born on the planet Trogon.

2. Mega Woman, Star Shark, and I will save this city ourselves!

3. You three can't take on the entire alien army yourselves!

4. It's clear that you yourself have the ability to lift a large building.

5. Zoe Fire herself defeated Evil Eye, the most dangerous villain ever.

6. I heard that Falcon himself fought the villains.

7. It looks like the members of Super League made their costumes themselves.

Read the sentence. Write an intensive pronoun to complete it.

8. You _____ have seen Zorloc's hidden fortress.

9. Galaxy Boy _____ caught the bank robber.

10. We will destroy the wormhole _____.

11. I _____ met several members of Super League.

The New Recruit

Read the story. Then write intensive pronouns for the underlined subjects. The first one has been done for you.

Skills:
Write intensive pronouns;

Use intensive pronouns;

Produce a sentence using an intensive pronoun

1.   Team Ultra recruited me, Starkid, last week.

You see, I ___myself___ have the ability to sense

danger before it happens. Samantha Storm called me

_____ and said, "Starkid, we here at Team Ultra protect the

world. But we can't always do it _____. You _____

foiled Dino Punk's plan to build the mega-ray. How about joining us?"

    I went to the Team Ultra headquarters. The building _____

doesn't look like much from the outside. Inside, however, I saw amazing

technology. Mac Brainwave designed the technology _____.

    Suddenly, I had a superhero vision. "Alien invaders are about to

attack Earth!" I exclaimed.

    "Impossible!" Mac said. "My equipment isn't picking up any signal."

    "They're coming through a wormhole," I said. "They built it

_____." The team followed up on my superhero information,

and it turned out that I was right. I even helped the team prevent the

aliens from invading. Afterward, I was part of Team Ultra!

Write a sentence using an intensive pronoun.

2. _____

_____

_____

Superheroes

Dashes and Parentheses with Nonrestrictive Elements

Use **parentheses** or **dashes** to set off nonrestrictive elements from the rest of a sentence. A **nonrestrictive element** gives extra information in a sentence. If a nonrestrictive element were removed from a sentence, the sentence would still be complete and make sense. You must always use two parentheses.

The mayor thanked Fiona Flame **(**the fearless superhero**)** for saving the city.

Use two dashes when the nonrestrictive element is in the middle of the sentence. Use one dash when the nonrestrictive element is at the end of the sentence.

The mayor thanked Fiona Flame—the fearless superhero— for saving the city.

Read the paragraph. Then write dashes to set off the nonrestrictive elements in the sentences.

New message	
To	**National Gazette**
Subject	**Advertisement**

1. Do you have any superpowers amazing speed, strength, or intelligence? If so, then we have a job for you! Bad Squad the evilest bunch of super villains in North America is actively seeking new recruits. We have some very exciting plans stealing junk food, turning people into zombies, and completing work on our tornado machine. All interested villains both amateur and professional are invited to apply.

Read the sentence. Write parentheses where they belong.

2. Fiona Flame who is an expert spy answered the ad.

3. She tricked the group's boss Doc Gruesome into thinking she was evil.

Heroes and Villains

Look at the pictures of the superheroes and villains. Read the description of each superhero. Then write an intensive pronoun in the sentence. Last, unscramble the bold letters to form the villain's name and complete the sentence.

Skills:
Write intensive pronouns;
Unscramble letters to form a word and complete a sentence;
Use visual information

1. Bolt Girl _____ defeated the

   ___ ___ ___   ___ ___ ___, plus

   many oth**e**rs.

2. **H**is **p**owerful super **cape** can fight vill**ain**s such as

   ___ ___ ___   ___ ___ ___ ___ all by

   _____ .

3. We _____ **h**arne**s**s **g**reat **p**owers

   to bea**t** the villain ___ ___ ___ ___ ___ .

4. You _____ **m**ust ru**i**n the evil pla**n**s of

   ___ ___ ___ ___   ___ ___ ___

   so h**e** **can't** win.

5. Athle**t**ic Man _____ **w**on against

   ___ ___ ___ ___ .

6. I _____ **ef**fortlessly extinguished

   the bl**a**ze of **m**y enemy, ___ ___ ___ ___ .

Superheroes

Skills:

Identify errors with intensive pronouns;

Identify punctuation errors with nonrestrictive elements;

Write sentences using intensive pronouns correctly;

Write sentences using dashes correctly;

Write sentences using parentheses correctly

Write It Right!

The following sentences have intensive pronoun errors and punctuation errors with nonrestrictive elements. Read the sentences carefully. Then rewrite the sentences correctly, adding dashes where they belong.

1. My supercar which can fly and go underwater uses the newest technology.

   _____

   _____

2. Zelgor itself is a clumsy villain his mistakes being well known by all.

   _____

   _____

3. She himself found what she was looking for the villain's hideout.

   _____

   _____

The following sentences have intensive pronoun errors and punctuation errors with nonrestrictive elements. Read the sentences carefully. Then rewrite the sentences correctly, using parentheses where they belong.
HINT End punctuation goes outside the parentheses.

4. Unfortunately, I yourself couldn't defeat Troga the enormous turtle monster.

   _____

   _____

5. You myself must stop Volt by tonight which is when he will shrink the city.

   _____

   _____

What's My Superpower?

Skills:
Write parentheses to set off nonrestrictive elements;
Write dashes to set off nonrestrictive elements;
Unscramble letters to solve a puzzle

Read the paragraph. Some sentences are missing punctuation. Write dashes or parentheses where they are needed.

My superhero name is Stealth Boy, and I have a lot of experience fighting crime. I defeated Agent Meanie who built a volcano machine. I stopped him before he used it the machine. Now he's in jail Star Galaxy Prison for life. Another villain Mr. Twister captured me. I escaped without him seeing me. I'm good at that because I practice. I heard a bank was robbed. The culprit turned out to be a new villain one of the worst villains. Arcto who uses an ice ray had just arrived in town. Her ice ray actually froze me once, but I thawed out. When she tried to rob the museum, I caught her because she didn't see me in time to freeze me. Her ice ray a dangerous device is now locked up. Another time, aliens invaded the city, but they didn't see me waiting for them. I appeared before they did any damage. My good friends also superheroes were with me. They my superhero friends help when there's a big problem. The mayor is calling me which means there's an emergency. I'm off to fight crime! See if you can figure out what my superpower is!

Superheroes

Follow the steps below to find out what Stealth Boy's secret power is.

1. How many sentences above did you have to add dashes or parentheses to? Write the number. _____

2. Add 2 to the number you wrote. This is how many letters are in the word that names Stealth Boy's superpower. _____

3. The word begins with an i and ends with a y. Unscramble the blue letters in the paragraph above to find the other letters in the word, and write the word on the line. _____

Helio to the Rescue!

Explain what an intensive pronoun is.

1. _____

_____

Write the eight intensive pronouns.

2. _____ _____ _____ _____

_____ _____ _____ _____

Explain how you can use parentheses and dashes in a sentence.

3. _____

_____

Write a sentence with an intensive pronoun.

4. _____

_____

Read the sentence. Write parentheses where they belong.

5. Helio who uses the energy of stars can travel anywhere in the universe.

6. The space-traveling hero drifts by his home planet called Omega 3600.

Read the sentence. Write a dash or dashes where they belong.

7. Helio receives a distress call from Team Ultra a superhero team from Earth.

8. The members of Team Ultra in desperate need of help cheer when Helio arrives!

Superheroes

Read the story.

The New Tent

Last weekend, my family headed to the forest for our favorite activity: camping! We picked a spot beside a lake. It was the perfect spot: peaceful, scenic, and comfortable. The ground was level, and there was diversity in the terrain: water, trees, and hills. The leaves above us provided shade, and we still had cellphone service, in case of an emergency. After picking the campsite, the next thing we had to do was obvious: set up camp! Mom and I grabbed supplies from the car while Manuel got to work on our new tent. I placed camp chairs around the fire pit, and Mom put the cooking gear on the picnic table. Manuel, meanwhile, was struggling with the tent. I helped Dad gather wood for a fire. Dad and Mom got a fire going and started cooking. And Manuel was still struggling with the tent! Various parts of the tent were strewn across the ground. By this time, Manuel was grunting and frustrated. At that point, Dad asked Manuel one question: "Do you need help?" Working together, they finally got the tent set up. As we all ate, Manuel laughed and joked about how he'd almost lost his taste for camping because of a tent!

Read the rules. Answer the questions.

Grammar A **prepositional phrase** shows the relationship between a noun or pronoun and another word in a sentence. Prepositional phrases can describe location, time, and other kinds of relationships.

FIND IT!

How many green prepositional phrases can you find in the story? _____

Punctuation We write a **colon** (:) after an independent clause to introduce an item or a list.

How many orange colons can you find in the story? _____

© Evan-Moor Corp. • EMC 9956 • Skill Sharpeners: Grammar and Punctuation

37

Concepts:
A prepositional phrase shows the relationship between a noun or pronoun and another word in a sentence;
A colon is used after an independent clause to introduce an item or list

Prepositional Phrases

A **prepositional phrase** is a group of words that shows the relationship between a noun or pronoun and another noun, or object, in a sentence. Prepositional phrases can describe location, time, and other kinds of relationships.

Location The family hikes **through the forest**.

Time We'll put up our tent **by dusk**.

Other Johan is going camping **with Lebron**.

Prepositional phrases always begin with prepositions. These words are prepositions:

above	on	along	around	at	toward
beside	with	for	from	out	up
into	under	across	by	through	between
over	in	off	below	down	inside

Skills:
Identify prepositional phrases;

Write a prepositional phrase;

Use a prepositional phrase;

Determine which prepositional phrase is appropriate to complete a sentence

The Great Outdoors

Read the sentence. Then underline the prepositional phrase.

1. My family spent a week camping in a cabin.

2. The rocky trail over Sourland Mountain is rather difficult.

3. While kayaking, Declan saw a painted turtle swim beneath the surface.

4. Willow's bike helmet is the one with all the stickers.

5. Dad found his childhood bicycle at Grandma's house.

6. Our guide for the trip was a canoeing expert.

7. We stuck our marshmallows into the fire.

Read the the prepositional phrases in the box. Then write the one that makes sense to complete the sentence.

| above the trees | under the low branches | through the trees |

8. Caleb made sure to duck _____.

Outdoor Fun!

A **prepositional phrase** always begins with a **preposition** and ends with **the object of the preposition**. A sentence can have one prepositional phrase or more than one.

preposition   object of the preposition

There is a large eel **under our raft**.

The preposition *under* shows the relationship of **location** between the "large eel" and "our raft."

Read the sentence. Underline each prepositional phrase.
Then circle the object of the preposition in each prepositional phrase.

1. Our instructor showed us the equipment we'll use for the climb.

2. Darius gripped the rock between his fingers.

3. Jamal hiked with Mikayla for hours around the lake.

4. Delilah and her sister took a selfie on the summit.

5. I helped Mom hang a hammock between two pine trees.

6. Max and his friends rode a speed boat across Lenape Lake.

7. Walking up the hill was not an easy feat for Ivan.

8. We faced our campsite toward the lake.

9. Georgette laid her sleeping bag beside her sister's sleeping bag.

Write a sentence about an activity you like to do outdoors.
Include a prepositional phrase in your sentence.

10. _____

_____

The Great Outdoors

Colons

Write a **colon** after an independent clause to introduce an item or a list of items. The list may have one item or more than one.

> There is only one thing I want to do today**:** play golf.
> We can play one of these games today**:** golf, volleyball, or softball.

We usually do not capitalize the first letter after the colon.
But we do capitalize the first letter if the list is one of the following:

- a complete sentence
- a quotation
- a formal statement or a general saying

Read the sentence. Then write a colon where it belongs.

1. I think you forgot an important piece of equipment your helmet.

2. The hike went through several ecosystems forest, meadow, and wetlands.

3. These are the reasons why I am exhausted We canoed.
   We hiked. We went rock climbing.

Read the sentence. Is the colon used correctly? Circle *yes* or *no*.

4. There's one thing I'll never do: skydive.   yes   no

5. I got: a new oar and new flippers.   yes   no

6. I need three things: sunscreen, a hat, and sunglasses.   yes   no

Read the sentence. Does it have correct capitalization after the colon?
Circle *yes* or *no*.

7. After our run, my brother said one thing: "that was fun!"   yes   no

8. I can't wait for our vacation: camping in Vermont!   yes   no

9. We did two things in Canada: We camped. We fished.   yes   no

Skill Sharpeners: Grammar and Punctuation • EMC 9956 • © Evan-Moor Corp.

On the Move

These kids are on the move! Look at the picture below.
For each person, write a sentence with a prepositional phrase.
You can use the prepositions provided or choose your own.

Skills:

Use visual
information;

Produce a
sentence with
a prepositional
phrase

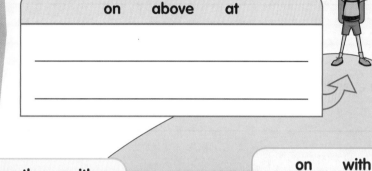

on	above	at
_____		
_____		

up	beneath	with
_____		
_____		

on	with	over
_____		
_____		

through	below	toward
_____		
_____		
_____		

with	beside	by
_____		
_____		
_____		

The Great Outdoors

Write It Right!

The sentences below have misplaced prepositions and colon errors. Read the sentences carefully. Then write them correctly.

1. The trails the mountain are tough on.

_____

_____

2. We have everything we need paddles, vests, and canoes.

_____

_____

3. "This is a long hike," Keisha said a tired voice with.

_____

_____

4. There were lots of obstacles the trail on roots, rocks, and a log.

_____

_____

5. Marie was being silly when she tried to row the river up!

_____

_____

6. Jake wants: to do three things He wants to swim. He wants to climb. He wants to fish.

_____

_____

Skill Sharpeners: Grammar and Punctuation • EMC 9956 • © Evan-Moor Corp.

Follow the Clues

The pictures below show what you saw on your hike. Write two journal entries that tell what you saw on the first day and the second day. Use a colon in each sentence.

Skills:
Use visual information;

Produce sentences correctly using colons to introduce lists;

Solve an alphabet code

Day 1

tree stump	squirrel	cave

_____

_____

Day 2

moose	pine cones	lake

_____

_____

The sentence below is written in code. Crack the code, and write the correct letters to read the sentence. **HINT** The last word in the sentence is **eagle**.

___ ___ ___ ___ ___ ___ ___ ___ ___ ___,
 m   l   m   s   p   f   g   i   c

___ ___ ___ ___ ___   ___ ___ ___
 u   c   q   y   u   y   f   y   u   i

___ ___ ___ ___ ___   ___ ___ ___ ___ ___.
 y   l   b   y   l   c   y   e   j   c

Get Outside!

Explain what a prepositional phrase is.

1. _____

_____

Explain how you can use a colon in a sentence.

2. _____

_____

Read the sentence. Rewrite the sentence using a colon.

3. During our hike, we saw three things, a lake, a boulder, and an eagle's nest.

_____

_____

Read the sentence. Underline the prepositional phrase. Circle the object of the preposition.

4. Elsa snapped the buckles of her life vest and then got her paddle.

5. Even though it was a cold night, it was toasty and warm inside the tent.

6. We got soaked when we stepped across the stream.

7. I pointed my glider toward the open field.

8. We managed to navigate our raft between the sharp rocks.

Write a sentence using a colon correctly.

9. _____

Skill Sharpeners: Grammar and Punctuation • EMC 9956 • © Evan-Moor Corp.

Read the story.

Instant Friends

Fiona came over on Saturday, and she brought her new puppy. At first, I was nervous. How would my big old dog, Bart, react to a puppy? **Bart might bark, or he might chase the puppy. I was worried, but it turns out I had nothing to be concerned about.** Our two dogs were instant friends.

"This is Pebbles," Fiona said. The little puppy yapped, jumped, and ran all over. **Bart didn't seem bothered by Pebbles' energy, nor did he mind it when she crawled over him.** Fiona and I watched as our two dogs ran around in my backyard. Pebbles romped and snapped at butterflies. Suddenly, the neighbor's dog, Sparky, barked from the other side of the fence. **Pebbles seemed scared, so Bart barked back at Sparky.** Then he licked Pebbles' nose. **Bart loves playing, yet he gets tired quickly.** He lay down for a nap. **Pebbles snuggled up against him, and she fell right to sleep.**

Read the rules. Answer the questions.

Grammar A **compound sentence** has two independent clauses, or two clauses that can each stand alone as a complete sentence, joined by a coordinating conjunction. These are the seven coordinating conjunctions: **for and nor but or yet so.**

How many blue **compound sentences** can you find in the story? _____

FIND IT!

Punctuation We write a **comma** (**,**) before the coordinating conjunction that joins the two independent clauses in a compound sentence.

How many orange **commas** can you find in the story? _____

Pets

45

Concepts:
A compound sentence has two independent clauses joined by a comma and a coordinating conjunction;
A comma is used before the coordinating conjunction in a compound sentence

Skills:

Identify compound sentences;

Identify coordinating conjunctions;

Identify each independent clause in a compound sentence

Compound Sentences

A **compound sentence** has two independent clauses, or clauses that can each stand alone as a complete sentence. Each clause is connected by a coordinating conjunction.

Independent clauses   Sandra wants a dog   her brother wants a cat

Compound sentence   Sandra wants a dog, **but** her brother wants a cat.

There are seven coordinating conjunctions.
Use FANBOYS to remember them.

F	A	N	B	O	Y	S
for	**and**	**nor**	**but**	**or**	**yet**	**so**

Read the sentence. Is it a compound sentence? Circle the answer.

1. Our new puppy is adorable, and it has a lot of energy.   yes   no

2. Django, my cat, spends the night in my room and wakes me up.   yes   no

3. Manny couldn't think of a name for his hamster, so I named it Earl.   yes   no

4. I saw a documentary about a guy who had a bear as a pet.   yes   no

5. The kitten runs all over but hides when the dog comes in.   yes   no

Read the compound sentence. Then circle the coordinating conjunction.

6. Having a pet iguana is so much fun, but it is also a lot of work.

7. My neighbor supposedly has a ferret, yet I've never seen it.

8. Fuyu has a pet bird, but her dad is the person who mostly takes care of it.

Read the compound sentence. Then underline the two independent clauses.

9. Rosa thinks fish are boring, but I like observing them.

10. We could take Walker on a hike, or we could go to the dog park.

11. I've always wanted a baby sloth as a pet, but they belong in a forest.

Skill Sharpeners: Grammar and Punctuation • EMC 9956 • © Evan-Moor Corp.

Pets

Pet Care

Read the pair of sentences. Then use them to write a compound sentence. Remember to write a coordinating conjunction in the sentence, and write a comma where it is needed.

1. Caring for a pet is a huge responsibility. It is a lot of fun.

   _____

   _____

2. I might give Sammy a bath today. I might wait until tomorrow.

   _____

   _____

3. Cody doesn't like raccoons. He always barks and growls at them.

   _____

   _____

4. My pet turtles play together. They love swimming in their aquarium.

   _____

   _____

5. My bird's name is Sweetie. She likes sitting on my hand.

   _____

   _____

Write a compound sentence. Remember to write a coordinating conjunction in the sentence, and write a comma before the conjunction.

6. _____

   _____

Pets

Commas in Compound Sentences

> In a compound sentence, write a **comma** before the coordinating conjunction that joins the two independent clauses.
>
> I just got a pet gecko, and it moves fast.
>
> My parents didn't want me to get a lizard at first, but they finally let me have one.
>
> I have to keep the lid on its tank, or it will get out.

Read the sentence. If it needs a comma, write a comma where it belongs.

1. Mom stops at the pet store for dog food so I go into the store with her.

2. A gerbil runs frantically on its wheel and then it gets a drink of water.

3. Perla's dog always sleeps in its bed or on the sofa.

4. I've heard that hedgehogs make good pets yet nobody I know has one.

5. My kitten jumps into my lap and it purrs loudly.

6. Yoko brings her dog to the park and does training exercises with it.

7. My fish, Mr. Rex, is colorful and interesting to look at.

Read the compound sentence. Does it have correct punctuation? Circle the answer.

8. We put our pet frog outside, and it hopped away.   yes   no

9. Our turtle may be small but it is as strong as an ox.   yes   no

10. Clive isn't a fan of cats, nor does he like dogs that much.   yes   no

11. Our family has a hermit crab and I help take care of it.   yes   no

12. The snake is sleeping right now, but it will move around later.   yes   no

13. I wouldn't want a pet snake, nor would I want a tarantula.   yes   no

Pets

What's Happening?

There are 15 fish in the aquarium. Use the words inside the fish to make 6 compound sentences. Write each sentence on a line, and remember to write a comma where it is needed.

Skills:

Use visual information;

Write compound sentences;

Form compound sentences

1. _____

2. _____

3. _____

4. _____

5. _____

6. _____

Pets

Write It Right!

The sentences below have errors. Some of the sentences have an incorrect coordinating conjunction. Some are missing a comma, and others have a comma but do not need one. Read the sentences carefully. Then write them correctly.

1. Surfer runs around and barks, nor he chews up our furniture!

2. My family doesn't have a pet right now nor I hope we'll get a kitten soon.

3. My gecko spends most of its time crawling, and standing in its pool.

4. I take Scruffy to the dog park or he gets plenty of exercise there.

5. The cat and dog seem to be fighting so they're actually just playing.

6. Feed the fish but do not overfeed it.

What Pet Should I Get?

Read the sentences, and write commas in the compound sentences where they belong.

Skills:
Write commas in compound sentences;

Distinguish between compound sentences that are missing commas and sentences that are not compound;

Unscramble letters to form words and solve a letter code

1. I'm getting a new pet but I haven't decided what kind I want.

2. I have two different animals in mind and will have to choose one.

3. I promised my parents I'd feed my pet and take good care of it.

4. They said we can go to the pet store on Saturday and pick out a pet.

5. I would be happy with either pet and I know that both pets will need attention.

6. This will be my first pet so I can hardly wait for the weekend to arrive.

7. We'll need some supplies and other things for my new pet.

8. We can buy the supplies at the pet store or we can order them online.

9. I've been reading about both animals and understand what they will need.

10. I spend time after school and after dinner reading or watching videos online.

11. My friend Chang will come over and we'll play with my pet.

12. Chang loves animals and has a pet snake of his own.

13. I know I have to wait until Saturday but it's going to be hard to wait that long!

On the lines below, write the green letters from the sentences you added commas to.

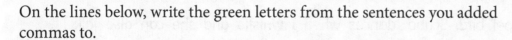
___ ___ ___ ___ ___ ___ ___ ___ ___ ___ ___ ___

What are the two animals that I may get as a pet? Unscramble the letters you wrote above. Write them to complete the sentence below.

I will get a _____ or a _____ .

Skills:
Write coordinating conjunctions;

Explain the function of coordinating conjunctions in compound sentences;

Explain how to determine whether or not a sentence is compound;

Identify compound sentences;

Write commas in compound sentences;

Produce a compound sentence

My Hamster

Write the seven coordinating conjunctions.

1. _____ _____ _____ _____ _____ _____ _____

Explain what a coordinating conjunction does in a compound sentence.

2. _____

_____

Read the sentence. Is it a compound sentence? Explain your answer.

3. Dad said we can get a hamster, but I'll be responsible for it.

_____

_____

4. Praline, my pet mouse, squeaks a lot.

_____

_____

Read the sentence. Then write a comma where it belongs.

5. Gouda is my neighbor's dog and he is the cutest dog I've ever seen.

6. Our pet bird, Scuba, dances when I whistle and she can also talk.

7. Our family has a pet tarantula and it eats insects.

Of all the animals in the world, decide which you would want as a pet. Write a compound sentence about it.

8. _____

_____

Concepts:
A complex sentence has a dependent clause and an independent clause joined by a subordinating conjunction;

A comma is used after the dependent clause when the clause is at the beginning of a complex sentence

Read the story.

Tough Competition

When the buzzer sounds, I take off. Another racer takes the lead. With my racing mitts on my hands, I furiously spin my chair's wheels and try to close the gap between me and her. I fly across the pavement **as** the crowd cheers.

I use a wheelchair **because** I have a joint condition. **Before** I got into racing, I spent a lot of time searching for a sport that I'd enjoy playing in my wheelchair. I am very competitive! **Whenever** I'm racing, I feel limitless and tough. I know I can do anything. When I race, I focus on just one thing: winning. **As** we approach the halfway point, my arms begin to tire. **Until** I reach the finish line, there's no slowing down! That girl is still in the lead. **Unless** I pick up the pace, she'll win. I go faster and faster, but it isn't enough. I come in just after her. **After** the race is over, she smiles and says I'm tough competition. I smile and tell her I'll be even tougher next time!

Read the rules. Answer the questions.

FIND IT!

Grammar A **subordinating conjunction** begins a dependent clause that joins an independent clause to form a complex sentence.

How many purple **subordinating conjunctions** and green complex sentences can you find in the story?

_____ **subordinating conjunctions**   _____ complex sentences

- -

Punctuation We write a comma (,) after the dependent clause when it is at the beginning of a complex sentence.

How many orange commas can you find in the story? _____

Sports

Subordinating Conjunctions

Skills:

Identify subordinating conjunctions;

Identify the independent and dependent clauses in complex sentences

A **subordinating conjunction** makes a clause dependent, so it cannot stand alone as a complete sentence. A subordinating conjunction is the first word in a dependent clause.

Independent clause   Nadia did some stretches

Dependent clause   before she raced

These words are subordinating conjunctions:

if	when	until	whenever
as	unless	because	wherever
after	although	while	before

Read the sentence. Then circle the subordinating conjunction.

1. Whenever our team plays the Thunderbolts, we wind up losing.

2. I practiced some dribbling skills while Dad got dinner ready.

3. I was completely exhausted after today's grueling practice.

4. Unless I have a totally clear shot, I'll pass the ball to Marco.

5. Rohan likes cross country more than track because she likes running far.

Read the sentence. Then circle the dependent clause, and underline the independent clause.

6. Coach told us to drink plenty of water before we begin practice.

7. Although it was cold during our game, all the running made me feel warm.

8. We'll be so excited if we win the championship.

9. My brother looks for new running trails wherever he goes.

10. As Bilal dribbled the ball, he zigzagged to avoid the opposing players.

Sports

Skill Sharpeners: Grammar and Punctuation • EMC 9956 • © Evan-Moor Corp.

Track and Field

A **complex sentence** is made up of a dependent clause and an independent clause. The dependent clause begins with a subordinating conjunction and can be at the beginning or the end of a complex sentence.

dependent clause
If the team wins the tournament, each member will receive a trophy.

dependent clause
Each member will receive a trophy if the team wins the tournament.

Read the sentence. Is it a complex sentence? Circle the answer.

1. After the school bell rang, Evie headed out to practice.   yes   no

2. Coach Emily led the team in a quick run around the track.   yes   no

3. If you miss too many practices, you can't compete in the meet.   yes   no

4. It was extremely hot today, so Kyle drank lots of water.   yes   no

5. Troy practiced long jumping until he couldn't jump any more.   yes   no

Read the sentence. Is it a complex sentence? Circle *yes* or *no*.
Then explain why you chose this answer.

6. After the school bell rang, Evie headed out to practice.   yes   no

_____

_____

7. The runners ran two laps, and Coach Emily tracked their time.   yes   no

_____

_____

Sports

Skills:

Write commas in complex sentences;

Distinguish between complex sentences that need commas and those that do not

Commas in Complex Sentences

> Write a **comma** after the dependent clause when it comes at the beginning of a complex sentence.
>
> After she watched the Olympics**,** Julie wanted to try snowboarding.
>
> When a dependent clause is at the end of a complex sentence, do not use a comma.
>
> Julie wanted to try snowboarding after she watched the Olympics.

Read the sentence. If it needs a comma, write a comma where it belongs.

1. Whenever she has time Monica goes to the ice rink to practice figure skating.

2. Haru can't wait until his family goes skiing in Colorado.

3. Wherever someone hits the puck Lea reaches it first.

4. Although there's no snow Damon can train for cross-country skiing.

5. Natalie's coach said Natalie could go to the Olympics someday if she keeps practicing.

6. Before Cody got into snowboarding he raced mountain bikes.

7. Camilla tried curling for the first time while she was visiting family in Norway.

8. Because the weather had been so warm skiing conditions weren't great.

9. After he'd practiced for a few days Sanjay felt confident snowboarding.

10. Martin and his family go skiing whenever they can get away for the weekend.

Sports

Soccer Practice

Today's soccer practice is tough! Read the sentences. Some sentences are complex, and others are not. To get the ball down the field, draw a line through all the complex sentences. Avoid any sentences that are not complex.

Skill:
Distinguish between sentences that are complex and sentences that are not complex

After school ends, I play soccer. Whenever I play soccer, I feel happy.

I have soccer practice.

Marco is our star player because he scores lots of goals. Although other sports are fun, soccer is the best.

Before I joined the school team, I played recreation soccer. If I play well, I can join the travel team.

I'm pretty good at playing soccer, but I'm not quite as good as Marco.

All my friends play soccer like I do.

I'm pretty good at playing soccer, but I'm not quite as good as Marco.

We practice passing, and then we go over some different plays.

Whenever I have time, I go into my yard and practice.

I didn't get into soccer until I was in third grade.

We'll work on passing after we work on dribbling.

With enough practice, I'm sure I'll get better at soccer.

Skills:

Identify comma errors in complex sentences;

Determine appropriate subordinating conjunctions to use in complex sentences;

Write complex sentences using subordinating conjunctions correctly;

Write complex sentences using commas correctly

Write It Right!

The sentences below have missing subordinating conjunctions and comma errors. Read the sentences carefully. Then write them correctly. You can use any subordinating conjunction that makes sense to complete each sentence.

1. _____ Owen gets close enough to the goal he takes a shot.

_____

_____

2. Coach sat us down for a huddle, _____ the long track meet began on Friday.

_____

_____

3. _____ the trail was rocky Katie flew down it like a pro.

_____

_____

4. Oliver and his brother run every day, unless there's lightning.

_____

_____

5. Dad said he'd pick up Nadine from tennis, _____ Mom had to work late.

_____

_____

6. _____ Jermaine is at a water polo match his sister is at volleyball practice.

_____

_____

Skill Sharpeners: Grammar and Punctuation • EMC 9956 • © Evan-Moor Corp.

Sports

Game Day!

It's the day of the big game. Let's get out there and give it our all! Rearrange the words in the balls so they form a complex sentence with correct punctuation. Write the new order of the words and punctuation on the line.

HINT Pay attention to capitalization.

Skills:

Write complex sentences;

Unscramble words to form complex sentences;

Use capitalization and punctuation as clues to determine the structure of a complex sentence

1

2

3

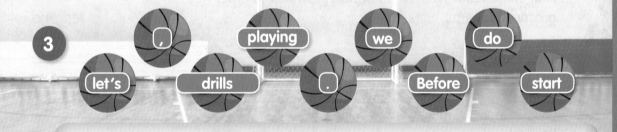

4

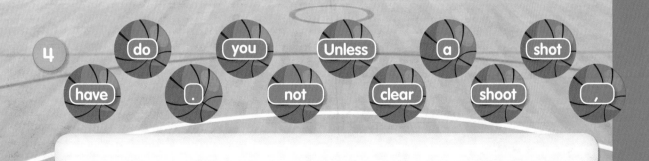

Skills:

Write subordinating conjunctions;

Explain what a complex sentence is;

Explain how to use a comma in a complex sentence;

Identify complex sentences;

Explain how to recognize complex sentences;

Distinguish between complex sentences and sentences that are not complex

Shooting Hoops

Write three subordinating conjunctions.

1. _____

_____

Explain what a complex sentence is.

2. _____

_____

Explain when a comma is needed in a complex sentence.

3. _____

_____

Read the sentence. Is it a complex sentence? Circle *yes* or *no*.
Then explain your answer.

4. Half of the team worked on dribbling while the other half practiced lay-ups.   yes   no

_____

_____

5. Wyatt thought quickly, and he passed the ball to his teammate Dita.   yes   no

_____

_____

6. As the other player took a shot, Milton jumped high to block it.   yes   no

_____

_____

Sports

Concepts:

Adverbs modify verbs, adjectives, phrases, clauses, and sentences and help describe how, when, and where;

A comma is used to separate each item in a series

Read the story.

Beach Day!

Saturday morning, I awoke **early**. I washed my face, brushed my teeth, and found my bathing suit. Then I went **outside** to help Dad. He was loading coolers, blankets, towels, and other gear into our car. My little sister, Eliza, was running **around**, **loudly** singing every "beach" word she knows. "Sand, waves, and seashells!" She **really** loves the beach. We go **frequently** in the summer, but this was the first time this season, and I don't think Dad had planned **well**. Mom came **over** and **carefully** examined everything. It turns out Dad hadn't packed snacks, water bottles, or extra clothes. We **quickly** gathered those items. Eliza, meanwhile, was **still** singing: "Flip-flops, clouds, and sharks!"

"That is **definitely** everything," he said **confidently**. We were now in the car and ready to go! Halfway down the driveway, Eliza sang, "Seabirds, sea stars, and sunscreen!" Dad stopped the car and laughed. "Thanks, Eliza! I **totally** forgot the sunscreen!"

Read the rules. Answer the questions.

Grammar   An **adverb** describes how, when, or where an action happens. Adverbs can also describe adjectives, phrases, and clauses.

FIND IT!

How many blue **adverbs** can you find in the story? _____

- -

Punctuation   Write a **comma** (**,**) to separate each item in a series. A series is a list of three or more items. Each item can be a single word or a phrase.

How many orange **commas** can you find in the story? _____

Skills:

Identify adverbs;

Recognize the functions of adverbs

Adverbs

An **adverb** describes how, when, or where an action happens. Adverbs can also describe adjectives, phrases, and clauses.

How	gently, easily, entirely, slowly, carefully
	Dylan **carefully** lifts the bucket, revealing a tower of sand.
When	regularly, now, frequently, later, hourly
	In the summer months, my family **frequently** visits the beach.
Where	here, there, far, inside, everywhere
	As Maisie runs, sand flies **everywhere**.

Read the sentence. Then circle the adverb or adverbs.

1. The dolphins jump gracefully out of the water.

2. Be sure to apply sunscreen regularly when the sun is out.

3. I go to the beach often, but I rarely see any whales.

4. During its migration, the humpback whale swims far.

5. If a shark appears here, the fish will quickly scatter.

6. My family always enjoys the beach.

Read the sentence. Does the underlined adverb describe **how**, **when**, or **where**? Circle the correct answer.

7. The sea turtle migrates <u>annually</u> in search of food.   how   when   where

8. The water looked so inviting that I had to jump <u>in</u>.   how   when   where

9. That big wave <u>totally</u> wiped out my sand castle.   how   when   where

10. I think we're planning to go to the boardwalk <u>later</u>.   how   when   where

11. I need you to stay <u>close</u> because the water is rough.   how   when   where

12. The angler fish lurks <u>silently</u> at the bottom of the ocean.   how   when   where

Skill Sharpeners: Grammar and Punctuation • EMC 9956 • © Evan-Moor Corp.

Ocean Life

Skills:
Form adverbs;
Write adverbs;
Use adverbs;
Produce a sentence using an adverb

You can form an adverb by adding -*ly* to some adjectives. Write an adverb using the adjectives below.

1. generous _____

2. rapid _____

3. amazing _____

4. luxurious _____

5. aggressive _____

6. cautious _____

Read the sentence. Then form an adverb from an adjective in the word box to complete the sentence.

> gentle   complete   vigorous   painful

7. Layla's sunburn looked _____ red and irritated.

8. Charity's beach ball bobbed _____ in the calm water.

9. All the kids covered Dad's legs _____ with sand.

10. Brandon splashed his brother _____ during their wave battle.

Write your own sentence about the ocean using an adverb.

11. _____

_____

Ocean

Punctuation Rule

Skill:
Write commas to
separate items in
a series

Commas with Items in a Series

Use **commas** to separate each item in a series, or list, of three or more items. An item can be a noun, a verb, an adjective, or another part of speech. A comma always goes before *and* or *or* in a series.

We saw crabs, pelicans, seagulls, and dolphins while at the beach today.

An item can be a single word or a phrase.

Series with words   blanket, umbrella, and cooler

Series with phrases   walk in the sand, splash in the waves, or lie in the sun

Read the series. Then write commas to separate the items in the series.

1. sunscreen sunglasses and flip-flops

2. swim splash or dive

3. take a walk go for a swim or nap on the blanket

4. float on a raft go out on a boat and surf the waves

5. arrived early spent the day on the beach and went to the boardwalk at night

Read the sentence. Then write commas to separate the items in the series.

6. Fish sea sponges and sea slugs can all be found in a coral reef.

7. A crab pinched me a wave knocked me over and a beach ball hit me.

8. The beach was dazzling peaceful and exhilarating.

9. I spent the day at the beach with my friends Diego Rupert Darcy and Chang.

10. We went snorkeling surfing and swimming today.

How Would You Do It?

Some adverbs describe how an action is performed. For example, you may read a book sleepily, eagerly, or fearfully. Look at the picture, and read the sentence. Then write four adverbs that you can think of to complete it. You can use adverbs from the word box or your own adverbs.

Skills:

Write adverbs;

Determine which adverb is appropriate in the context of a sentence;

Use visual information

fearfully	cheerfully	lazily	rapidly
gladly	vigorously	regularly	calmly
willingly	skillfully	painfully	nicely
rudely	hungrily	elegantly	foolishly

1

If I was swimming in the ocean and saw this, I would swim away _____.

_____   _____

_____   _____

2

I would _____ swim with dolphins.

_____   _____

_____   _____

3

I would _____ dive and explore this deep-sea shipwreck.

_____   _____

_____   _____

Ocean

Write It Right!

The sentences below have adverb errors and comma errors. Read the sentences carefully. Then write them correctly.

1. The ship chugs slow out of the harbor into the bay and out to sea.

   _____

   _____

2. Captain Tokkien nervous steers his ship through uncharted waters.

   _____

   _____

3. The coral reef has strange plants bizarre fish and colorful rocks.

   _____

   _____

4. The penguin skillful dives down hunts fish and escapes from a seal.

   _____

   _____

5. The air is cool salty fishy and refreshing.

   _____

   _____

6. The surfer stands effortless on his board and glides smooth over the waves.

   _____

   _____

Skill Sharpeners: Grammar and Punctuation • EMC 9956 • © Evan-Moor Corp.

Ocean

Marine Life Riddles

Each sentence below contains a series of items. Write commas to separate the items in the series. Then unscramble the green letters to find the answer to each riddle.

Skills:
Unscramble letters to form words;

Write commas to separate items in a series

1. I am a black-and-white marine animal a swimming mammal and a skilled hunter in the ocean.

___ ___ ___ ___

2. I have eight arms a beak a siphon and the ability to camouflage myself.

___ ___ ___ ___ ___ ___ ___

3. I float gently through water look like jelly and deliver a sting.

___ ___ ___ ___ ___ ___ ___ ___

4. I am a kind of shark that has gorged on manta rays birds sea snakes and even license plates.

___ ___ ___ ___ ___ ___ ___ ___

5. I have pincers antennae five pairs of legs and a snail's shell that I'm borrowing.

___ ___ ___ ___ ___ ___ ___

6. I have a long snout four fins bony plates and a tail that can grab things.

___ ___ ___ ___ ___ ___ ___

BONUS Create your own riddle that includes a series. Make sure all the letters you need for the answer are included in your sentence, and circle them.

7. _____

Answer to your riddle: _____

Ocean

© Evan-Moor Corp. • EMC 9956 • Skill Sharpeners: Grammar and Punctuation

Sailing Across the Sea

Explain what an adverb does in a sentence.

1. _____

_____

Write a sentence about the ocean or the beach. Include a series of items in your sentence, and use correct punctuation.

2. _____

_____

Write a sentence with an adverb that tells *how*.

3. _____

_____

Write a sentence with an adverb that tells *when*.

4. _____

_____

Write a sentence with an adverb that tells *where*.

5. _____

_____

Skill Sharpeners: Grammar and Punctuation • EMC 9956 • © Evan-Moor Corp.

Read the story.

Work Hard, Play Hard!

Ebony could see the neighbor kids' heads popping up above the fence each time they jumped on their trampoline. They were screaming and laughing. "Their backyard is more entertaining than ours," she thought. Her dad was in the military, and her family had just moved here. In the past year, the family had lived in Pensacola, Florida; San Diego, California; and Tacoma, Washington. For the past three days, Wednesday, September 15; Thursday, September 16; and Friday, September 17, Ebony was doing homeschool. But today was Saturday, the **most enjoyable** day of the week, so Ebony was planning to play outside—after she did chores. She put her laundry in the hamper. She washed dishes and put them away. This house's cupboards were narrower than the ones in the last house. Then she swept the kitchen. It was the **dustiest** floor she'd ever swept. After chores, Ebony happily told her mom she was going out to play. Pretty soon, Ebony had met Dale and Jada, the neighbors, and joined them on their trampoline. It was the **most bouncy** trampoline she'd ever been on. And Ebony's screams were the **loudest** of all!

Read the rules. Answer the questions.

Grammar We use comparative adjectives to compare more or less, usually between two nouns. We use **superlative adjectives** to compare the most or least between three or more nouns. Some comparative and superlative adjectives are a single word, and some are two words.

How many green comparative adjectives and blue **superlative adjectives** can you find in the story?

_____ comparative adjectives

_____ **superlative adjectives**

FIND IT!

Punctuation We write semicolons **;** to separate items in a series when at least one item has a comma within it.

How many orange semicolons can you find in the story? _____

© Evan-Moor Corp. • EMC 9956 • Skill Sharpeners: Grammar and Punctuation

Concepts:
Comparative adjectives compare more or less of a quality, usually between two nouns. Superlative adjectives compare most or least of a quality between three or more nouns;

Semicolons are used to separate items in a series when an item has punctuation

Chores, chores, chores!

Comparative and Superlative Adjectives

chores, chores, chores!

> **Comparative adjectives** compare more or less between two or more people, places, animals, or things. Many comparative adjectives end in **-er**.
>
> It will be **cheaper** to repair the washer than to buy a new one.
>
> **Superlative adjectives** compare the most or least between three or more people, places, animals, or things. Many superlative adjectives end in **-est**.
>
> This is the **toughest** stain I've ever had to remove.

Read the sentence. Then circle the adjective. On the line, write *comparative* or *superlative* to tell which kind of adjective it is.

1. This detergent makes the clothes cleaner than the other one. _____

2. These are the sturdiest clothespins I've ever used. _____

3. My brother's room is messier than my room. _____

4. This spray removes even the dirtiest stains. _____

Read the sentence. Is the underlined adjective comparative or superlative? Circle the answer. Then explain why you chose the answer you did.

5. This is the <u>gentlest</u> sponge that the store sells.   comparative   superlative

_____

_____

6. The blue rag is <u>thicker</u> than the pink one.   comparative   superlative

_____

_____

Scrubbing and Polishing

Skills:
Distinguish the appropriate way to form comparative and superlative adjectives;

Form comparative and superlative adjectives;

Produce sentences using comparative and superlative adjectives

You can form some comparative adjectives by writing *more* or *less* before the adjective or by adding **er**. Read the adjective. Then write the comparative form of it.

1. powerful _____
2. stubborn _____
3. expensive _____
4. bubbly _____
5. neat _____
6. tiring _____

You can form some superlative adjectives by writing *most* or *least* before the adjective or by adding **est**. Read the adjective. Then write the superlative form of it.

7. frustrating _____
8. tiny _____
9. excited _____
10. broad _____
11. fragrant _____
12. polished _____

Write a sentence using a comparative adjective that uses the word *more* or *less*.

13. _____

_____

Write a sentence using a superlative adjective that uses the word *most* or *least*.

14. _____

_____

chores, chores, chores!

Semicolons with Items in a Series

Skills:

Write semicolons to set off items in a series;

Produce a sentence using semicolons to set off items in a series

A series is a list of three or more items. We usually write commas to separate each item in a series. When an item has a comma within it, we write a **semicolon** (**;**) to separate each item.

> Vernon, my brother**;** Asia, my sister**;** and Naomi, my friend, are helping me clean up this huge mess.

> We repainted the house on October 7, 2016**;** October 8, 2017**;** and October 9, 2018.

Write a semicolon before the word **and** or **or** in the series.

Read the sentence. Then write semicolons to separate the items in the series.

1. Each time we moved, on May 6, 2018 July 7, 2018 and December 12, 2018, we had to clean the house we were leaving.

2. Diane, a teacher Yoko, an actress and Latoya, a lawyer, do chores.

3. Chen, a personal trainer Tyrone, a chef and Vince, an author, live together and divide the chores.

4. If you lived in Nairobi, Kenya Surat, India or Hohhot, Mongolia, your daily chores would probably be much different than they are.

5. On June 19, 2017 June 20, 2017 and June 21, 2017, we thoroughly bathed all our dogs.

6. Mrs. Cooly, our neighbor Mr. Potts, my teacher and Dr. Fine, our doctor, are helping us build a patio.

7. Vinny, my uncle Kara, my aunt and Pearl, my cousin, can't relax until they've washed all the cars in their driveway.

Write a sentence with a series that requires semicolons to separate each item.

8. _____

_____

Skill Sharpeners: Grammar and Punctuation • EMC 9956 • © Evan-Moor Corp.

Swanson Family Chores

Skills:
Use logic to answer a question;

Identify comparative and superlative adjective errors

The Swanson family members share household chores. Each person does only one chore. Read the clues and look for errors in comparative or superlative adjectives. Cross out any clue with an error — it will lead you to the wrong answer. Use the remaining clues to figure out which chore each person does. Write **X**s in the grid to show which chores each person does **not** do. Write **Y**s in the grid to show which chore each person **does** do.

	Cutting grass	Washing dishes	Mopping	Ironing	Dusting
Mom					
Dad					
Ken					
Kate					
Aunt Lana					

1. According to Dad, the more enjoyable chores of all require soap and water.

2. Kate found a dirty plate and accused Ken of doing the worse job ever.

3. Aunt Lana's hands are more delicate than Dad's, so she avoids doing dishes.

4. Kate is happier in the kitchen than the yard, so she does her chore there.

5. Cutting the grass is the lengthiest chore of all the family's chores.

6. Mom is the more willing person in the entire family to do the ironing.

7. Aunt Lana uses the finest ironing skills in her chore.

8. Mom believes cutting the grass is the most entertainingest of all the chores.

9. Dad must do his chore outside when the temperature is cooler.

10. Ken uses a feathery tool and becomes the least sweaty when he does his chore.

11. Kate is carefuller than Mom at mopping.

12. Mom makes the floor the cleanest part of the house.

Chores, chores, chores!

Write It Right!

The sentences below have comparative and superlative adjective errors and errors with semicolons in a series. Read the sentences carefully. Then write them correctly.

1. Paul, your brother Drake, your cousin and James, your uncle are the more talented people ever at cleaning drains.

_____

_____

2. We have to clean out the pool on May 28, 2021 May 29, 2021 and May 30, 2021.

_____

_____

3. Children's chores in the 1800s were probably difficulter than they are now.

_____

_____

4. Dad worked at stores in Chicago, Illinois Tulsa, Oklahoma and Akron, Ohio.

_____

_____

5. The more miserable chore of all is cleaning the oven.

_____

_____

6. Betsy thinks cleaning the refrigerator is most enjoyable than dusting furniture.

_____

chores, chores, chores!

Teddy's Big Mess

Teddy used too much soap when he did the laundry! Read the words and punctuation marks on the bubbles in order. They form sentences with series. Write an **X** to cross out the bubbles that have inappropriate semicolons.

Skills:
Identify inappropriate semicolons in sentences;

Identify correctly placed semicolons in a series

Teddy's mom and Jillian saw the huge mess Teddy made, and they came up with a solution so that this kind of mess never happens again. To find out their solution, use the green words in the bubbles. Unscramble the green words to form a sentence that tells the answer. Write the sentence below.

_____

_____

chores, chores, chores!

Things We Have to Do

Explain the difference between comparative and superlative adjectives.

1. _____

_____

_____

Explain when you should use semicolons to separate items in a series.

2. _____

_____

Read the sentence. Circle the comparative or superlative adjective. Then write *correct* or *incorrect* to indicate whether the sentence uses the comparative or superlative adjective correctly.

3. Brody did the more sloppy job I've ever seen when he tried to vacuum. _____

4. Sharice hung up the brightest sheets on the clothesline. _____

Read the sentence. Then write semicolons to separate the items in the series.

5. On March 19, 2021 March 20, 2021 and March 22, 2021, we will clean the entire attic.

6. When we lived in Hamburg, Germany Kyoto, Japan and Wuhan, China, we always had daily chores to do.

Write a sentence with a superlative adjective.

7. _____

_____

Skill Sharpeners: Grammar and Punctuation • EMC 9956 • © Evan-Moor Corp.

A History of Clothing

One defining trait is that **we** wear clothing and other species do not. Taking this for granted, we put on clothes every day but rarely stop to think about when or how clothes were created in the first place. Historians believe that people have been wearing clothes for over 170,000 years, and **they** used leaves and animal skins. To be protected from harsh weather conditions, early people started using other materials such as bark and fur. Interestingly, there is evidence that a sewing needle made of bone was used 40,000 years ago, and **it** is primitive. Statuettes from the Paleolithic era, 30,000 to 10,000 BCE, shows women wearing items. This is further evidence that clothing was worn in prehistoric times. By the time Queen Elizabeth I took the throne in England in 1558, clothing styles were as trendsetting and distinctive as they are today. Queen Elizabeth I was known for wearing large stiffened gowns, for example, and her mother, Anne Boleyn, was known for wearing a French hood. **She** was admired for her beauty and style. As you know, we do not dress the same way today as people did in the 1500s. **It** is always evolving. Who knows what people will be wearing in a hundred years?

Read the rules. Answer the questions.

Grammar   A **vague pronoun** is a pronoun that does not have a clear antecedent or that has more than one possible antecedent. It should be clear which noun the pronoun is referring to.

How many purple **vague pronouns** can you find in the text? _____

FIND IT!

Punctuation   We write a **comma** (,) to separate an introductory element from the rest of a sentence. An introductory element is a word, phrase, or clause that is before the main clause of a sentence.

How many orange **commas** can you find in the text? _____

Concepts:
Pronouns should refer to a single clear antecedent;
Commas are used to set off an introductory element from the rest of a sentence

History

Vague Pronouns

A **vague pronoun** is a pronoun that does not have a clear antecedent, or noun that it refers to.

The carriage carried only the president's wife, as **they** were traveling separately.

A pronoun is also vague if there is more than one antecedent that it could refer to.

<u>George Washington</u> was the first U.S. president, and <u>Abraham Lincoln</u> was the sixteenth president.

He is written about in many history books.

Read the pair of sentences. Then circle the vague pronoun.

1. In the American Civil War, General Robert E. Lee was a confederate leader, and Ulysses S. Grant was a Union army leader. He later became a U.S. president.

2. The Civil War was fought between the Northern states and Southern states. They won the war in 1865.

3. You can use a library or the Internet. It has many resources about the war.

4. When the Civil War began, the Southern states had a population of 9 million, and the Northern states had a population of 22 million. After the war, many of them were lost.

5. Confederate Brigadier General Samuel Garland and Union Brigadier General Robert McCook died in 1862. The Battle of South Mountain was fatal for him.

Read the pair of sentences. Circle the vague pronoun. Then underline the two unclear antecedents that the circled pronoun may refer to.

6. Mary Todd Lincoln worked as a volunteer nurse in Union hospitals, and Clara Barton was a Civil War nurse who helped pass supplies to soldiers in the field. She saw a lot of wounded soldiers.

7. The American Revolutionary War took place from 1775 to 1783, and the Civil War took place from 1861 to 1865. It was a victory for President Abraham Lincoln.

History

Unclear Antecedents

A **vague pronoun** is a pronoun that does not have a clear antecedent because there is either no matching antecedent at all or there is more than one possible antecedent.

> Some historical rulers worked together, and **it** inspires some current rulers.

> <u>King Henry VIII</u> and <u>King Francis I</u> hosted a summit together, and **he** feasted for weeks.

Another kind of vague pronoun error occurs when the antecedent of a possessive adjective or possessive pronoun is unclear.

> Kat Ashley was the chief lady in waiting to Queen Elizabeth I, and **she** was **her** role model.

Read the sentence. Then circle the possessive adjective or possessive pronoun that has an unclear antecedent.

1. Abe Lincoln's friend Joshua Speed recalled how funny his stories were.

2. After Mahatma Gandhi died, Henry Polak remembered his peaceful protesting for human rights.

Mahatma Gandhi

3. Queen Mary I had a bitter rivalry with her half-sister, Queen Elizabeth I, and claimed that the rule of England was hers.

Read the sentence. Then explain why the underlined pronoun is vague.

4. Marie Antoinette told Anne d'Arpajon that <u>she</u> needed to leave the royal court.

_____

_____

5. A five-year-old boy named Cooper wrote a letter to former U.S. president George H. W. Bush to say that broccoli is good for <u>him</u>.

_____

_____

History

Skills:

Write commas to set off introductory elements;

Produce a sentence with an introductory element using correct punctuation

Commas to Set Off Introductory Elements

Write a **comma** to separate an introductory element from the rest of the sentence. An introductory element is a word, phrase, or clause that comes before the main clause of the sentence. The main clause is the part of the sentence that can stand alone as a complete sentence.

To research a history topic, you can find reliable sources online.

introductory element   main clause

Read the sentence. Then write a comma to separate the introductory element from the rest of the sentence.

1. Throughout most of its history China was ruled by powerful families, or dynasties.

2. Fighting for equal rights brave women throughout history have worked for a woman's right to vote.

3. Their traditions being important to them many immigrants have tried to observe their birth countries' customs in their new countries.

4. Historically the U.S. has been known as a "melting pot" because it has welcomed immigrants from many different nations.

5. In the Middle Ages people ate many foods that we do not choose to eat today.

6. For many people learning about the history of other countries is fun.

Write a sentence about history. Include an introductory element in your sentence, and use correct punctuation.

7. _____

History

Vague Pronoun Bingo

Skills:
Identify vague pronoun errors;

Unscramble letters to form a word and solve a puzzle

Read the sentences in the bingo card below. Color the squares that have vague pronoun errors. Also color any square in which a possessive adjective or pronoun has an unclear antecedent.

BINGO

Georgia told her mom that she has a stain on her shirt.	Eun-Jung says she wants to stay at the museum longer.	Nick and his friends saw Haruto and his friends at the museum, but they weren't staying long.	Corbin and his dad visited the history museum, but he became bored quickly.
Sophie loved seeing the ancient mummy exhibit at the museum. They made the mummy's tomb look authentic.	Jaden and Mike ran into their history teacher at the mall.	Irene insists to her sister that the antique is hers.	Mrs. Wen is at the museum with her family, and they are interested in the history exhibit.
Mr. Webber, our history teacher, shows our class photos of artifacts.	Otis told Jeremy that the history textbook was his.	My history teacher says that he used to be an archaeologist.	Naomi promised Chelsea that she could see the mummy.
Frank told Mario that his history test was on the table.	Ricardo and Dan gasped when they saw the mummy.	Ursula couldn't wait to hear the history experts' speeches. It was going to be interesting.	Felipa can't find her dad, so she asks the museum staff to page him on the speaker.

Look at the first letter in each square that you colored above. Unscramble the letters to form a word, and find the answer to the question below.

What word best describes vague pronouns? _____

History

Skills:

Identify missing commas with introductory elements;

Identify vague pronoun errors;

Correct vague pronoun errors;

Write sentences with commas to set off introductory elements

Write It Right!

The sentences below have vague pronouns and missing commas with introductory elements. Read the sentences carefully. Then write them correctly. To correct a vague pronoun error, write a noun or pronoun to replace the vague pronoun in your sentence.

1. Because they had no refrigerators in the Middle Ages people often dried foods.

   _____

   _____

2. People would use a foot or tail in a stew to make it tasty.

   _____

   _____

3. To make food appealing some chefs in the Middle Ages put the feathers back on birds after roasting them.

   _____

   _____

   _____

4. During wartime food options were sometimes limited.

   _____

   _____

5. Known as the person who invented airtight food preservation Nicolas Appert was a chef.

   _____

   _____

History

History Report Clues

Each student in Ms. Lee's class wrote a history report on the same topic. Read the sentence on each report below. Then write a comma to separate the introductory element if it is needed.

Skills:
Write commas to set off introductory elements;

Unscramble letters to form a word and solve a puzzle

In medieval times the wealthiest people did this more often than other people.

For centuries natural herbs, oils, and ashes were used because they had a strong smell.

Before soaking water had to be collected and heated over a fire.

Saving water an entire family would often share one tub of water to do this.

Queen Isabel I is believed to have done this activity only twice in her life.

When they did not have enough water to cover themselves entirely people would use wet rags to do this activity.

To avoid the spread of illness people washed their hands with vinegar and warm water in medieval times.

In ancient times people went to houses that were made for this activity.

Households in medieval times did not have plumbing or running water, as we do today.

What history topic is Ms. Lee's class writing reports about? The sentences above provide a clue. Unscramble the blue letters above to form a word, and find the answer. Write it below.

Ms. Lee's class is writing about the history of _____.

History

Skills:

Explain what a vague pronoun is;

Explain what an introductory element is;

Write commas to set off introductory elements;

Identify vague pronouns;

Explain vague pronouns in context

History

Explain what a vague pronoun is.

1. _____

   _____

Explain what an introductory element is.

2. _____

   _____

Read the sentence. Then write a comma to separate the introductory element from the rest of the sentence.

3. Fortunately for historians there are many different eras in history that can be studied.

4. While some historians like to work at historical sites many historians would rather teach history than study old artifacts.

5. In college you can study different aspects of history if you choose to.

Read the pair of sentences. Circle the vague pronoun. Then explain why the pronoun is vague.

6. You can study world history, African-American history, labor history, Asian history, and more. It is valuable.

   _____

   _____

7. Your history book probably has a chapter about World War II. You may find it interesting.

   _____

   _____

Concepts:

A sentence's subject and verb should agree in number;

Titles of books, movies, and TV shows are italicized or underlined

Read the story.

The Natural Gamer

Dillon and his friends Shasta and Waldo **have been playing** video games in Dillon's room. Dillon's little brother, Ernie, **walks** in and says, "I want to play, too." Dillon **rolls** his eyes and **begins** to walk Ernie out of the room.

"I'll put on *Pillow Monsters* for you," **says** Dillon. "It's your favorite movie."

"Aw, let him play," **says** Shasta. "He can create a me-person!" In the video game, a me-person is an avatar, or a character that looks like a cartoon character, that you design and control. You can decide what color hair it **has**, what it **wears**, and what its name is. Dillon and his friends **help** Ernie make one and show him how to use the controller. It doesn't take long.

Afterward, Ernie **asks** if he can play the game. "This game might be scary for you," says Dillon. "Are you sure you wouldn't rather read *Fluffy Tales*? Ernie **insists** on playing. Soon, he is vigorously pressing buttons and rotating the joystick on the controller. Shasta and Waldo **cheer** Ernie on.

After one round, an exhausted Ernie **hands** the controller to a grumpy-faced Dillon. "I got a score of 786," says Ernie. "Is that good?" Shasta and Waldo quickly **inform** Ernie that he **has beaten** Dillon's high score. "Awesome!" **exclaims** Ernie. "I'll go watch *Comet Rangers* now. Bye!"

Read the rules. Answer the questions.

Grammar A sentence must have **subject-verb agreement**. This means that a singular subject requires a singular verb, and a plural subject requires a plural verb.

How many purple **verbs** in sentences with **subject-verb agreement** can you find in the story? _____

Punctuation Titles of books, movies, or TV shows should be **typed in italics** or **underlined**.

How many orange **titles typed in italics** can you find in the story? _____

FIND IT!

Gaming

Subject-Verb Agreement

A sentence must have **subject-verb agreement**. This means that a singular subject requires a singular verb, and a plural subject requires a plural verb.

Incorrect	Correct
Ana **win** the game.	Ana **wins** the game.
Tito and Demetri **scores** points.	Tito and Demetri **score** points.
She **buy** a new game.	She **buys** a new game.

Read the sentence. Circle the incorrect verb. Then write it correctly on the line.

1. Nadia grow crops in her farming video game. _____

2. Mitch and Connor plays a racing game. _____

3. Kotori earn a new high score. _____

4. Pamela and her brother fixes the game controller. _____

Read the sentence. Complete it with the present tense form of the verb that is below the line. Make sure that the verb agrees with the subject.

5. Every time we play this game, it _____.
   freeze

6. The company _____ this game series every two years.
   update

7. All my friends _____ this game.
   own

8. Keith and Miranda _____
   with each other.   compete

Gaming

Skill Sharpeners: Grammar and Punctuation • EMC 9956 • © Evan-Moor Corp.

What a Realistic Game!

Skills:
Write a verb to ensure subject-verb agreement;

Distinguish between sentences with correct and incorrect subject-verb agreement;

Explain subject-verb agreement in context

When a subject has two parts joined by *and*, it takes a plural verb.

The animals **and** the people in this game **appear** so realistic.

When a subject has two parts joined by *or*, the verb must agree with the second part of the subject.

Either the bear **or** the walrus **jumps** out in that part of the game.

Either the shark **or** the crabs **try** to snap at you in this game.

Read the sentence. Complete it with the present tense form of the verb that is below the line. Make sure that the verb agrees with the subject.

1. The avatars and the background _____ like they're real.
   seem

2. A monster or a fairy _____ you in the fifth level of the game.
   help

3. The house or the trees _____ to move in the game.
   begin

4. Pritty and Deeta _____ the game every time they play.
   beat

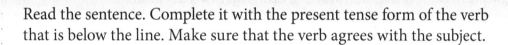

Read the sentence. Does it have subject-verb agreement?
Circle the answer. Then explain why you chose the answer you did.

5. Tobias and Honda thinks the characters in this game are scary.   yes   no

_____

_____

6. The game features avatars with realistic facial expressions.   yes   no

_____

_____

Gaming

Skills:

Underline titles of books, movies, and TV shows;

Produce sentences with titles using correct punctuation;

Identify titles with missing punctuation

Punctuation of Titles: Books, Movies, and TV Shows

Underline the title of a book, movie, or television show.

Mom reads <u>The Willow Tree</u> while Dad and I play a video game.

After we played a video game, we watched the movie <u>Tangled</u>.

My sister watches <u>Shaun the Sheep</u> on TV while I play a game.

If you are typing a title, use *italics* for the title.

We watched *Moana* after playing our fitness video game.

Read the sentence. Then underline the title or titles in the sentence.

1. My sister loves the movie Frozen as much as I love my new video game.

2. The new game I just bought is based on the TV show called Arthur.

3. In the movie The Wizard, a boy is amazing at playing video games.

4. A film called The Angry Birds Movie is based on a video game.

5. I watched The Super Mario Bros. Super Show! many years ago.

6. When Pablo saw the movie Sonic the Hedgehog, he loved it.

Write a sentence about a book you have read in the past year. Use correct punctuation.

7. _____

_____

Write a sentence about a movie you have watched in the past year. Use correct punctuation.

8. _____

_____

Skill Sharpeners: Grammar and Punctuation • EMC 9956 • © Evan-Moor Corp.

So Many Avatars!

Skills:
Write verb phrases;

Ensure subject-verb agreement;

Use visual information

Look at the video game picture. Then write a verb phrase to complete each sentence, and tell what is happening in the picture. Use a different verb in each sentence, and make sure each sentence has subject-verb agreement.

1

The boy and the dinosaur _____

_____

_____

_____.

2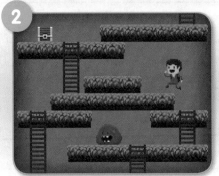

A monster _____

_____

_____

_____.

3

The people playing this game _____

_____

_____

_____.

4

The car _____

_____

_____

_____.

Gaming

Write It Right!

The sentences below have subject-verb agreement errors and title punctuation errors. Read the sentences carefully. Then write them correctly.

1. Mojgan and Roya plays a game based on the book Rapid Flotation Race.

   _____

   _____

2. Jakwon or Kim win this game every time.

   _____

   _____

3. Ceaser loves the movie The Golden Compass, and he also likes the game.

   _____

   _____

4. This game have puzzles and clues and are based on the TV show Spy Kids.

   _____

   _____

5. All these games is familiar because I've played them before.

   _____

   _____

6. My brother attempt to play a new video game every week.

   _____

   _____

Skill Sharpeners: Grammar and Punctuation • EMC 9956 • © Evan-Moor Corp.

Design a Video Game

There are so many different kinds of video games!
Follow the steps below to create your own video game.

1. Choose a theme for your video game. You can choose a theme from the words below, or you can choose your own theme.

| kitchen | safari | evil scientist | race |

Theme: _____

2. Write a description of your video game. Tell about the main character and what the character must try to do to win the game. (For example, is your character trying to save someone, find ancient relics, or grow crops on a farm?)

Description: _____

_____

3. Now draw a scene from your video game. You can draw your main character, a building, a villain, or background features of your game.

4. Pretend that your video game is being turned into a movie, a book, and a TV show! Write a title for each, and use correct punctuation.

Movie Title: _____

Book Title: _____

TV Show Title: _____

Games, Movies, Books, and TV

Explain what subject-verb agreement is.

1. _____

_____

Write a sentence telling what your favorite TV show is. Use correct punctuation.

2. _____

_____

Write a sentence telling what your favorite book is.
Use correct punctuation.

3. _____

_____

Write a sentence telling what your favorite movie is. Use correct punctuation.

4. _____

_____

Read the sentence. Does it have subject-verb agreement? Circle the answer. Then explain your answer.

5. All the stores in this town sells the same video games.   yes   no

_____

6. The avatars in this game move quickly.   yes   no

_____

Gaming

Skill Sharpeners: Grammar and Punctuation • EMC 9956 • © Evan-Moor Corp.

Read the text.

Astonishing Animals

If you **think** the animal world is fascinating, then you **are** not alone. Many people **write** stories, songs, and poems about the animals they **love**. The poem "T Is for Tarsier" by Liz Brownlee, for example, kindly **describes** the tarsier. And "BlobFish Dance Song" is only 30 seconds long, but it still **manages** to convey the most popular opinion about the blobfish: that it's ugly. In fact, many people find the blobfish interesting enough to write about. The article "Behold the Blobfish" **demonstrates** this fact.

The tarsier is a tiny primate in Asia, and it **has** humongous eyes. These cute creatures **spend** their lives in dense forests, away from humans. The blobfish, on the other hand, is notable because it was voted "the world's ugliest animal" in 2013. Some people **say** it looks sad because its mouth **turns** downward, like a frown. The blobfish is from the deep sea and probably **looks** similar to other fish in its natural environment; however, above water, it **appears** slimy, like pink jelly.

There is a wide world of beautiful (and ugly) animals to learn about.

Read the rules. Answer the questions.

Grammar An **inappropriate shift in verb tense** occurs when the verb tense in a sentence or paragraph changes without a reason. We write verbs in the same tense unless there is a reason to change it.

How many blue **verbs** can you find in the text? _____

FIND IT!

Punctuation We write **quotation marks** " " around titles of songs, poems, articles, and short stories. We always use quotation marks in pairs.

How many pairs of orange **quotation marks** can you find in the text? _____

Inappropriate Shifts in Verb Tense

> Verb tense tells when an action happens. An **inappropriate shift in verb tense** occurs when the verb tense in a sentence or paragraph changes without a reason. This can make it confusing to know when something happens.
>
> **Incorrect**   In 2018, scientists **discovered** new species and **name** them.
>
> **Correct**   In 2018, scientists **discovered** new species and **named** them.
>
> We usually keep the verb tense the same to avoid confusion.

Read the sentence. Circle the two verbs in the sentence.
Are the verb's tenses the same? Circle *yes* or *no*.

1. The capybara is noteworthy because it will be the largest rodent on Earth.   yes   no

2. The capybara grows to 3.2–4.2 feet (100–130 centimeters) long and weighs 60–174 pounds (27–79 kilograms).   yes   no

3. Some people compare the capybara to the hippo because they both had barrel-shaped bodies.   yes   no

4. The capybara is a herbivore and had been eating only vegetation.   yes   no

5. Capybaras live in groups, and each group will contain about ten members.   yes   no

Read the sentence. Are the verb's tenses the same?
Circle the answer. Then explain your answer.

6. Capybaras are active during dawn or dusk, but they will be active at night, too.   yes   no

_____

_____

Animals

Endangered Animals

An **inappropriate shift in verb tense** occurs when the verb tense in a sentence or paragraph changes without a reason. This can make the sentence or paragraph confusing. You can shift the verb tense if there is context in the sentence and the change in verb tense makes sense.

Inappropriate shift	The Endangered Species Act **passed** and **helps** animals.
Appropriate shift	The Endangered Species Act **passed** in 1973 and still **helps** animals today.

Read the sentence. Then rewrite it in the present tense to correct the verb tense error.

1. The black rhino was a beautiful animal that is critically endangered.

_____

_____

Read the sentence. Then rewrite it in the past tense to correct the verb tense error.

2. Mountain gorillas were discovered in 1902, but their population decreases shortly after.

_____

_____

Read the sentence. Is there an inappropriate shift in verb tense? Circle the answer.

3. Efforts will continue so that, one day, no more orangutan species were endangered. yes no

4. An animal conservation group declared that the Mexican grizzly bear becomes extinct in 1982. yes no

Animals

Punctuation of Titles: Songs, Poems, and Short Stories

Write **quotation marks** around the title of a song, poem, article, or short story. We usually write other common punctuation marks, such as commas and periods, inside the quotation marks as well.

"Anaconda" is the theme song of the movie with the same name.

"Baby Tortoise" is an old poem.

"The Bees and the Beetles" is a short story about how people are different from one another.

Read the sentence. Then write quotation marks where they belong.

1. The theme song to the movie *Jaws* is called Theme from Jaws.

2. The poem The Parakeets is entertaining for adults and children.

3. The Lion and the Elephant is an uplifting short story.

4. In one movie, a gorilla loves the song California Dreamin'.

5. The Pesky Fly is a humorous poem written in limerick form.

6. The Tortoise and the Hare is a short story with an important moral.

Write a sentence that includes the title of a song, poem, article, or short story that you like. Remember to use correct punctuation.

7. _____

_____

_____

_____

Shifty Verb Tenses

Skills:

Identify inappropriate shifts in verb tense;

Unscramble letters to form a word and solve a puzzle

Read the paragraph. Underline the sentences with an inappropriate verb tense shift.

Tons of people think that sharks attacked people constantly. A report claims that vending machines injure more people every year than sharks do. One animal that is more likely to attack is the crocodile because it caught its prey both in the water and on land. Crocodiles blended in perfectly with their environment, so they will be difficult to spot. They cause about 1,000 human deaths a year. Perhaps the most deadly animal is the mosquito, though, which will contribute to about 725,000 human deaths per year. Even though these statistics are true, we do not have to fear all animals. Just remember that many animal attacks happen when people will enter an animal's environment. We must have respect for all animals, especially when we are on their turf.

Read the first letter of each sentence you underlined. Then write each letter on a line below.

___ ___ ___ ___ ___ ___

For each letter you wrote, find the letter that comes before it in the alphabet. (For example, if you wrote a Q, you would find the letter P.) Write each new letter below.

___ ___ ___ ___ ___ ___

Unscramble the last row of letters you wrote to form the name of a mystery animal. Write it below.

Animals

_____

Skills:

Identify inappropriate shifts in verb tense;

Identify titles with missing punctuation;

Write sentences with titles using correct punctuation;

Correct inappropriate shifts in verb tense

Write It Right!

The sentences below have verb tense shifts and missing punctuation with titles. Read the sentences carefully. Then write them correctly.

1. The Ape and the Carpenter is a funny story with a lesson.

_____

_____

2. The lion stalks its prey, and then it pounced on the prey in a burst of speed.

_____

_____

3. The sloth is a herbivore and ate leaves from many different kinds of trees.

_____

_____

4. Blackbird is a catchy song, which the Beatles record in 1968.

_____

_____

5. The Day Dreaming Jackal teaches that it is best to think twice before acting.

_____

_____

6. I like The Trickster Monkey when I read it last year.

_____

_____

Animals

I Recommend This Title...

You volunteer at the children's library, and today the kindergarten class is coming in to read. You have made copies of songs, poems, and short stories on little sheets of paper. Some kindergartners have brought in a picture of an animal they like. Use the picture to recommend a song, poem, or short story for each kindergartner. Then complete the sentence, and use correct punctuation when you write titles.

Skills:
Use visual information;

Write titles of songs, poems, and short stories using quotation marks;

Use inference

Songs
| If You Should Meet an Elephant |
| Kookaburra Sits in the Old Gum Tree |
| Slippery Fish |

Poems
| Goosey, Goosey Gander |
| Crabby |
| A Lion's Roar |

Short Stories
| The Tortoise and the Hare |
| The Lion and the Mouse |
| The Man and the Little Cat |

1

I think you would like _____

because _____.

2

I think you would like _____

because _____.

3

I think you would like _____

because _____.

4

I think you would like _____

because _____.

Animals

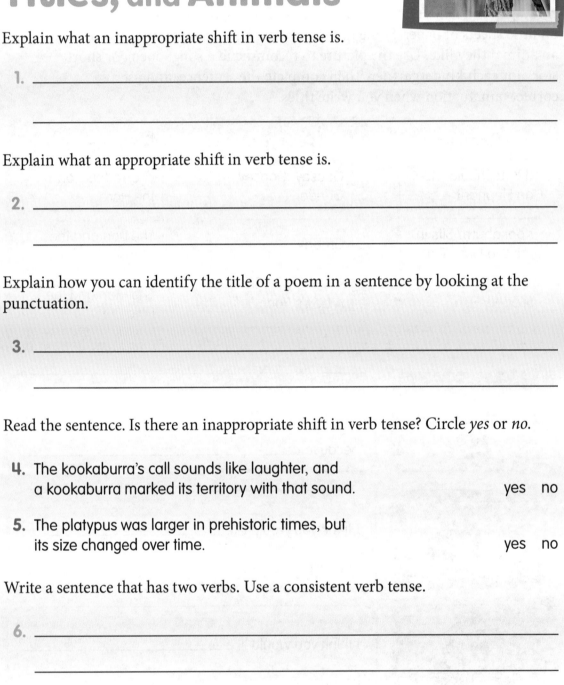

Verb Tenses, Titles, and Animals

Explain what an inappropriate shift in verb tense is.

1. _____

_____

Explain what an appropriate shift in verb tense is.

2. _____

_____

Explain how you can identify the title of a poem in a sentence by looking at the punctuation.

3. _____

_____

Read the sentence. Is there an inappropriate shift in verb tense? Circle *yes* or *no*.

4. The kookaburra's call sounds like laughter, and a kookaburra marked its territory with that sound.   yes   no

5. The platypus was larger in prehistoric times, but its size changed over time.   yes   no

Write a sentence that has two verbs. Use a consistent verb tense.

6. _____

_____

What is your favorite song? Write a sentence telling what it is, and use correct punctuation.

7. _____

_____

Read the story.

The Unusual Breakfast Smoothie

"Hey, Mom," hollered Sydney from the living room, "what are you putting in our breakfast smoothie this morning?" Sydney was super hungry.

"Well, why don't you come here and help me make it, Syd!" Mom shouted back. A moment later, Sydney was watching Mom chop a pineapple. "We ran out of yogurt," Mom said. "No worries! I know you like your yogurt, but I'll use coconut milk this morning. Trust me, you'll like it!"

Sydney could see freshly washed berries in the blender. She also saw coconut milk, chopped kale, and pieces of lemon and avocado. "Okay, Mom," Sydney said thoughtfully, "let's try it. And Dad will probably like it, too, because he loves coconut." She smiled as she grabbed three cups from the cupboard—they were the special breakfast smoothie cups. Just then, Sydney had a wild idea. "Mom, since you and I are changing up the smoothie this morning anyway," she began, "can we add some jalapeño to it?" Mom loved the idea. The smoothie was sweet and spicy. Yum!

Read the rules. Answer the questions.

Grammar An **inappropriate shift in pronoun** occurs when pronouns that disagree in number, gender, or point of view are used to refer to a single antecedent.

How many green antecedents and blue **pronouns** can you find in the story?

FIND IT!

_____ antecedents   _____ pronouns

Punctuation We write a **comma** ⟨,⟩ and a pair of **quotation marks** ⟨"⟩ ⟨"⟩ to set off a speaker's words in a story.

How many orange commas and pairs of quotation marks can you find in the story?

_____ commas   _____ quotation marks

Healthy Lifestyle

Concepts:
An inappropriate shift in pronoun occurs when pronouns that disagree in number, gender, or point of view are used to refer to a single antecedent;

A comma and quotation marks are used to set off a speaker's words

Avoiding Inappropriate Shifts in Pronouns

An **inappropriate shift in pronoun** occurs when a pronoun does not agree with other pronouns with the same antecedent. Pronouns referring to a single antecedent must agree in **number**.

Incorrect	When **someone** cooks, **they** should use sanitary methods.
Correct	When **someone** cooks, **he or she** should use sanitary methods.

Pronouns referring to the same antecedent must agree in **gender**.

Incorrect	**Someone** usually gardens when **he** has a green thumb.
Correct	**Someone** usually gardens when **she or he** has a green thumb.

It is okay to use the same pronoun or pronouns more than once to avoid inappropriate shifts.

Read the sentence, and circle the pronouns. Then write *number* or *gender* to describe the pronoun error.

1. Mom uses them daily because it is fresh. _____

2. It is crisp, and you can taste them. _____

3. She cooks healthy meals at home because he enjoys cooking. _____

Read the sentence. Then rewrite it to correct the inappropriate shift in pronoun.

4. Someone tried it, and they didn't like it.

_____

_____

Healthy Lifestyle

Getting Active

Pronouns referring to the same antecedent must agree in **person**.
Pronouns can be in the first, second, or third person.

| Incorrect | When **someone** uses heavy weights, **you** should have a spotter. |
| Correct | When **someone** uses heavy weights, **she or he** should have a spotter. |

Skills:
Identify pronouns;
Correct inappropriate shifts in pronouns

Read the sentence with the underlined antecedent. Circle the pronoun that shifts inappropriately. Then write the correct pronoun to replace the one you circled.

1. When <u>someone</u> is a vegetarian, you do not eat meat. _____

2. When <u>I</u> jog, you love doing it outside. _____

3. <u>Everyone</u> likes to jog outside because we like the fresh air. _____

4. Whenever <u>we</u> exercise, they make a lot of noise. _____

Read the sentence. The antecedent is underlined. Rewrite the sentence to correct the inappropriate shift in pronoun.

5. <u>Everybody</u> needs physical activity so we can be fit and healthy.

_____

_____

6. <u>You</u> exercise energetically when we eat nutritiously.

_____

_____

Healthy Lifestyle

Skills:

Write quotation marks and commas in dialogue;

Write a sentence using quotation marks and commas in dialogue;

Use quotation marks correctly with end punctuation

Commas and Quotation Marks with Dialogue

Write **commas** and **quotation marks** to set off a quotation in dialogue, or a speaker's exact words in a conversation. Write quotation marks before and after the exact words. Write a comma before or after the exact words. End punctuation and commas usually go inside the quotation marks.

> Floyd says, "I add nuts and raisins to my oatmeal."
>
> "We need more bananas," Luis tells his mom.

When words interrupt the quotation, write commas and quotation marks to set off only the speaker's exact words.

> "If we don't have blueberries," says Nia, "we'll use strawberries."

Read the sentence. Then write commas and quotation marks where they belong.

1. Getting plenty of sleep says Dr. Burr is important for good health.

2. I feel like I have more energy after I exercise said Eduardo.

3. I love making salad said Cole because I can put any vegetable in it.

4. When I crave a dessert claims Lupita I like vanilla yogurt with fruit.

5. Hugh exclaimed I never thought I'd like cabbage, but I do!

Read the sentence. Then rewrite it with commas and quotation marks where they belong.

6. Amelia says Even though I sprained my ankle, I can still exercise.

_____

_____

Skill Sharpeners: Grammar and Punctuation • EMC 9956 • © Evan-Moor Corp.

Healthy Lifestyle

Pronoun Shift Coded Message

Read each sentence, and identify the inappropriate pronoun shift. Then find the letter code of the appropriate word or words in the box. On the line, write the letter that matches the correct pronoun or pronouns for the sentence.

o = I	t = you	m = he or she	h = it	s = he	p = she	a = we
u = they	r = me	k = him or her	y = him	f = her	n = us	b = them

1. It's important for anyone to include fruits and vegetables in his or her diet so you can have good nutrition. _____

2. He says that she believes a nutritious diet, a good night's sleep, and physical activity are important for good health. _____

3. They study food's impact on human health, and we often give people advice about food, too. _____

4. When a person becomes a nutritionist, they study food science. _____

5. A food allergy can be severe, and they should be taken very seriously. _____

6. I ate all of them, and it was delicious. _____

What is Sunita's favorite snack? Read the letters you wrote above. Then unscramble the letters to form a word, and find the answer.

7. Sunita's favorite snack is _____.

Have you ever eaten hummus? If you have, write a food that you like to eat with hummus. If you do not like hummus or have not tried it, write your favorite snack.

8. _____

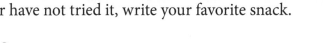

Healthy Lifestyle

Skills:
Identify inappropriate shifts in pronoun;
Determine appropriate pronouns to use in sentences;
Correct inappropriate shifts in pronoun;
Unscramble letters to form a word and complete a sentence

Write It Right!

The sentences below have inappropriate pronoun shifts and missing punctuation to set off quotations. Read the sentences carefully. Then write them correctly. You may need to write different pronouns to correct the pronoun errors.

1. Swimming is great exercise said Mr. Brown because it's easy on joints.

   _____

   _____

2. When someone wants to live a healthy lifestyle, they have many food options.

   _____

   _____

3. She figured out that he wants to eat a vegan diet.

   _____

   _____

4. Mark drinks water a lot because she knows it's very beneficial.

   _____

   _____

5. Some people take vitamins to supplement their diets said Dr. Griffin.

   _____

   _____

6. Stan can have dessert said Mom if you read this health article first.

   _____

   _____

Skill Sharpeners: Grammar and Punctuation • EMC 9956 • © Evan-Moor Corp.

Who Enjoys This Meal?

Each sentence below has a quotation. Some of the sentences have correct punctuation to set off the quotation, but some of the sentences have missing punctuation or punctuation in the wrong place. Circle the sentences with correct punctuation.

1. Ellie claims, "I am allergic to peanuts, and those lettuce wraps have peanut sauce on them."

2. Guillermo says "I will not eat anything green," but "I like a lot of other nutritious foods".

3. "I read that turmeric has health benefits, said Regan, so I put that spice in my chicken soup.

4. "When eggplant is roasted," states Pedro, "and topped with pomegranate and walnuts, the flavor is out of this world."

5. Lettuce wraps "are my favorite food ever said Bridgette."

6. "Crisp iceberg lettuce is my favorite lettuce to use for lettuce wraps," says Tyson.

7. "Creamy pumpkin soup is my favorite," says Jennifer, "especially when it is topped with toasted pine nuts."

Use only the sentences with correct punctuation as clues to figure out who enjoys each meal shown below. Write the name of the person who enjoys the meal on the line below the picture.

_____   _____   _____

Skills:
Use visual information;

Identify sentences with correct punctuation to set off quotations;

Identify sentences with missing punctuation to set off quotations;

Use context clues to answer a question

Skills:

Explain what an inappropriate pronoun shift is;

Identify the ways that a pronoun must agree with an antecedent;

Explain how to use punctuation to identify quotations in dialogue;

Identify inappropriate shifts in pronoun;

Produce a sentence with a quotation using correct punctuation

Wellness

Explain what an inappropriate pronoun shift is.

1. ____

____

Read the sentence. Then fill in the bubbles beside all the words that can correctly complete the sentence.

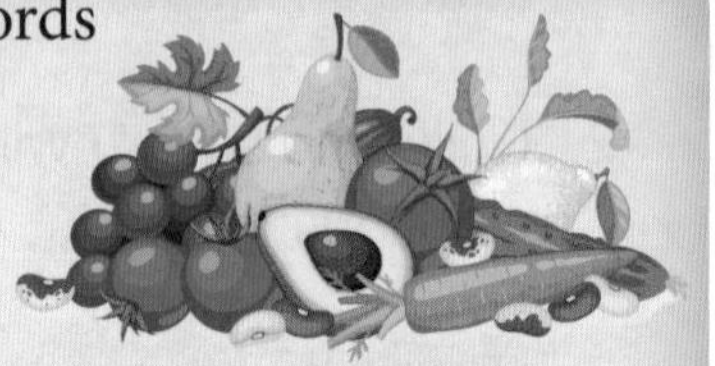

2. A pronoun must agree in ______.

O length	O gender	O spelling	O appearance
O position	O number	O person	O name

Explain how you can identify a speaker's exact words when you are reading a story.

3. ____

____

Read the sentence. Does the bold pronoun agree with the underlined antecedent? Circle the answer.

4. <u>Frank</u> eats a balanced diet because **she** wants to be healthy. yes no

5. When <u>people</u> exercise, **they** can strengthen their hearts and other muscular organs. yes no

6. The health choices <u>a person</u> makes may be different when **they** are a teenager from when **they** are an adult. yes no

Write a sentence with a quotation. Use correct punctuation.

7. ____

____

Healthy Lifestyle

Read the story.

Dominic's Magic Teacher

When Dominic's parents took Dominic to see the marvelous, spellbinding magic show of Enchanting Evelyn, he became obsessed with the art of illusion. He needed to know how Enchanting Evelyn did her spooky, fantastic tricks. She could disappear in a puff of smoke, lift a mammoth red garbage truck twenty feet into the air with a flick of her sparkly, shimmering wand, and turn a woman into a bunny. Dominic spent hours online reading about many ancient ways to create illusions, and he read about modern, sophisticated techniques, too. But he still couldn't figure out how Enchanting Evelyn did her magic. So he begged his parents to take him to more incredible magic shows. Dominic's parents were impressed with how dedicated he was to his surprising new hobby, so they agreed. One night, while Enchanting Evelyn was performing, he snuck backstage. He saw a young, adorable frog. Suddenly, the frog started talking! It said, "Thank goodness you noticed me sitting here! Let's go onstage. Enchanting Evelyn isn't the only one who can do magic tricks!" Dominic was shocked that the frog knew magic.

"Tell me everything you know!" exclaimed Dominic.

"Okay," the frog agreed, "but first, I'm hungry! Do you have any flies?"

Read the rules. Answer the questions.

Grammar An adjective describes a person, place, animal, or thing. There is a specific order of adjectives when they appear together to modify the same noun. These are called cumulative adjectives.

FIND IT!

How many green adjectives can you find in the story? _____

Punctuation We write a comma (,) between coordinate adjectives. Coordinate adjectives appear together to provide details that are equally important about the same noun.

How many orange commas can you find in the story? _____

© Evan-Moor Corp. • EMC 9956 • *Skill Sharpeners: Grammar and Punctuation*

Concepts:
Cumulative adjectives are usually placed in a specific order within a sentence;

A comma is used to separate coordinate adjectives

Skill:
Identify the correct and incorrect order of cumulative adjectives in sentences

Order Adjectives Within a Sentence

Adjectives provide facts and opinions about nouns. Adjectives can describe size, number, color, and more. The words **a**, **an**, and **the** are adjectives called *determiners*. When adjectives before the noun provide <u>different kinds of details</u>, they are called **cumulative adjectives**, and we put them in a specific order.

The mysterious tall French magician vanished into thin air.

When adjectives are in order, they do not need commas between them. This is the **order of adjectives:**

1. determiners	**2.** number	**3.** opinion	**4.** size	**5.** age
6. shape	**7.** color	**8.** origin	**9.** material	**10.** function

Read the sentence. Then write *correct* if the adjectives are in the correct order. Write *incorrect* if the adjectives are not in the correct order.

1. The magician pulled out five adorable little rabbits from his hat. _____

2. Nicole did an outrageous new card trick. _____

3. The experienced French two illusionists perform street magic. _____

4. She ripped green a crisp rectangular dollar bill into pieces, and her wand made it whole again. _____

5. He made the Siberian white ferocious large young tiger completely disappear. _____

6. The three nervous young volunteers slowly walked onstage. _____

7. She performed in a humongous circular auditorium. _____

8. He performed dangerous four tricks. _____

Magic Show

What Magicians Do

Skills:
Produce sentences using at least three cumulative adjectives;

Order adjectives correctly within a sentence;

Use visual information

This is the **order of adjectives:**

1. determiners   2. number   3. opinion   4. size   5. age
6. shape   7. color   8. origin   9. material   10. function

The magician draped **a large rectangular black silk** cape over the chair.

TIP: Read the sentence aloud to make sure that the order of adjectives sounds correct.

Look at the picture, and write a sentence describing the picture. Use at least three adjectives before a single noun in your sentence, and put the adjectives in the correct order.

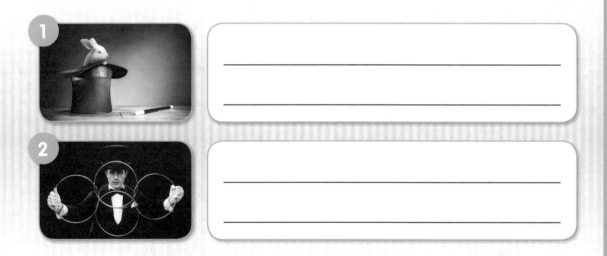

The sentences below have adjectives in the wrong order.
Rewrite the sentence with the adjectives in the correct order.

3. Gray tiny seven doves flew out of his hat.

_____

4. She made valuable antique a car disappear.

_____

Magic Show

Commas with Coordinate Adjectives

Write a **comma** between coordinate adjectives. When adjectives before a noun provide <u>similar kinds of details</u> or are equal in importance, the adjectives are coordinate.

The wand released a **sweet, fragrant** bouquet of lilies into the air.

The adjectives "sweet" and "fragrant" are coordinate because they both provide a sensory detail about the smell of the noun *bouquet*.

TIP: Switch the positions of the adjectives. If the sentence still sounds correct, then write a comma between the adjectives.

Read the sentence. Then write a comma to separate the coordinate adjectives.

1. The Great Majikeenee was a clumsy careless magician.

2. His flimsy weak props often fell apart onstage.

3. When he tried to guess someone's secret hidden card, he always got it wrong!

4. Once, he meant to release a rabbit, but he released a frightening dangerous snake instead.

5. His devoted loyal assistant became injured during a show.

6. His unhappy disappointed audience always left feeling unimpressed.

Write a sentence with coordinate adjectives. Use correct punctuation.

7. _____

_____

Magic Show

Magic Bubbles

Read the words in the bubbles. Follow the bubbles that form a sentence with adjectives in the correct order. Color each circle that you pass through from **Start** to **End**.

Skills:
Identify a sentence with cumulative adjectives in the correct order

Magic Show

Write It Right!

The sentences below have adjectives in the wrong order and are missing commas between coordinate adjectives. Read the sentences carefully. Then write them correctly.

Skills:

Identify errors in the order of cumulative adjectives;

Identify missing commas with coordinate adjectives;

Write sentences with commas to separate coordinate adjectives;

Order cumulative adjectives correctly within a sentence

1. The whimsical bizarre magician swooped over the astonished audience.

   _____

   _____

2. The oval wooden old large stage was not strong enough to hold all the props.

   _____

   _____

3. The magician performed with a blazing sizzling light display on the stage.

   _____

   _____

4. Gregorio learned magic from outstanding veteran an European illusionist.

   _____

   _____

5. Melissa began doing simple manageable card tricks when she was a child.

   _____

   _____

6. Vernon the Talented is a famous brilliant magician who does difficult many illusions.

   _____

   _____

Magic Show

Skill Sharpeners: Grammar and Punctuation • EMC 9956 • © Evan-Moor Corp.

Skills:
Use visual information;

Produce sentences using commas to separate coordinate adjectives;

Describe optical illusions

Is It Really Magic?

Each picture below is an optical illusion. Look at the picture. Then describe what you see in the picture or why you think the picture is unusual.

1

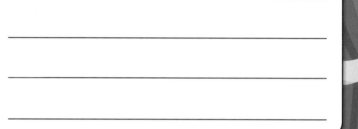

_____

_____

_____

_____

2

_____

_____

_____

_____

Write a sentence about picture number 1 above. Use coordinate adjectives in your sentence, and use correct punctuation.

3. _____

Write a sentence about picture number 2 above. Use coordinate adjectives in your sentence, and use correct punctuation.

4. _____

Magic Show

Magic Show!

Skills:

Explain what coordinate adjectives are;

Explain a method to check that adjectives are in the correct order;

Identify coordinate adjectives;

Write commas to separate coordinate adjectives;

Identify sentences with cumulative adjectives in the correct and incorrect order

Explain what coordinate adjectives are.

1. _____

_____

Explain why you may want to read a sentence aloud when it has multiple adjectives together.

2. _____

_____

Read the sentence. Then write a comma to separate the coordinate adjectives.

3. With a wave of the wand, the nervous shaken volunteer disappeared from the stage.

4. When the magician's unsuccessful failed trick was over, the audience groaned.

5. I have never seen such a daring risky performance before.

Read the sentence. If the adjectives are in the correct order, write *correct* on the line. If the adjectives are not in the correct order, rewrite the sentence correctly.

6. The metal creepy enormous gray rectangular cage floated above the stage.

_____

_____

7. The cheerful retired German magician enjoys watching other magicians perform.

_____

_____

Magic Show

Read the text.

The Amazing World of Science

Some facts are so surprising that they seem more like fiction. **Did you know that bees could count, for example?** Researchers in Australia have trained bees to count**, but** the bees could count only to four. Want more startling facts? Octopuses have three hearts. **And unless you have saliva in your mouth, you cannot taste the flavor of food.** Interestingly, people have known for centuries that hot water can freeze more quickly than cold water**;** scientists are still not completely certain why it happens, though. How do we know all these astonishing facts? **Science is the reason! Centuries of research, experimentation, and observation have helped humans develop technology, build structures, make medicine, and gain information about Earth and outer space.** There are different science domains**.** Physical science is the study of natural objects and forces. **Life science is the study of living things, and Earth science focuses mainly on the study of Earth and its atmosphere.** We are fortunate**;** we all benefit from the work of scientists.

Concepts:

Varied sentence patterns include different structures, lengths, subjects, and vocabulary;

There are multiple ways to correct a run-on sentence, including using a semicolon, splitting the sentence into two sentences, and creating a compound sentence

Read the rules. Answer the questions.

Grammar   A text with **varied sentence patterns** has different kinds of sentences with different lengths, subjects, and word choices.

How many purple sentences with **varied sentence patterns** can you find in the text? _____

- -

Punctuation   These are some of the ways to correct a run-on sentence. You can write a **period and capital letter** to make two sentences. Or you can write a **semicolon** to separate the two independent clauses. A third way is to write a **comma and coordinating conjunction** to make a compound sentence.

FIND IT!

How many orange **corrections for run-on sentences** can you find in the text? _____

Science

Varied Sentence Patterns

The term **sentence pattern** refers to a sentence's structure, or how a sentence is built. For example, the most basic sentence patterns are **subject-verb** and **subject-verb-object**.

Subject-verb pattern	A scientist types.
Subject-verb-object pattern	A scientist types notes.

A text with **varied sentence patterns** has sentences with different **lengths**, **subjects**, and **word choices**. Varied sentences usually make a text more interesting than a text with only short or only long sentences.

No varied patterns	The scientist types. The scientist observes. The scientist researches.
Varied patterns	The scientist types notes. An exciting new discovery has been observed, and it needs to be documented. There is still important research to do!

Read the short paragraph. Then circle *varied* or *not varied* to describe the sentence patterns.

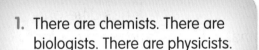

1. There are chemists. There are biologists. There are physicists.

   varied   not varied

2. You may think that all scientists work in a lab, but not all of them do! There are countless types of jobs for scientists. Many scientists even enjoy teaching.

   varied   not varied

3. Realizing which branch of science is particularly interesting is important for a scientist. In fact, it's crucial. Many scientists enjoy their careers, for they're interested in their work.

   varied   not varied

4. Scientists may work in a lab. Scientists may work in the field. Scientists may work for a school.

   varied   not varied

Skill Sharpeners: Grammar and Punctuation • EMC 9956 • © Evan-Moor Corp.

Scientists

Skill:
Write sentences with varied sentence patterns;

Write a compound sentence;

Write a simple sentence;

Use a coordinating conjunction

You can **vary sentence patterns** by using different kinds of sentences. These are some of the kinds of sentences you can use:

Simple	Some scientists study sleep.
Compound	Scientists may work in medicine, or they may work with rocks.
Complex	Before they found salts on Mars, scientists didn't know Mars had ever had water on it.
Compound-complex	When they froze and then unfroze worms, scientists discovered that the worms kept their memories, and this discovery was surprising.
Interrogative, or a question	Does Mars have glaciers?

Read the sentences. Then rewrite them as one compound sentence. Use a comma and the coordinating conjunction **and**.

1. Some scientists study insects. Some scientists study fish.

_____

_____

Read the sentences. Then rewrite them as one simple sentence.

2. A scientist may study earthquakes. A scientist may study the weather.

_____

_____

3. Scientists help us make medicine. Scientists help us preserve food.

_____

_____

Science

Punctuation to Correct Run-on Sentences

A **run-on sentence** has two or more sentences that are joined together without correct punctuation or a conjunction. Below are some of the ways to correct the following run-on sentence:

Sea horses don't have stomachs they eat constantly.

Use a **period** and a **capital letter** to split the sentence into two.

Sea horses don't have stomachs**.** **T**hey eat constantly.

Use a **semicolon** to separate the independent clauses.

Sea horses don't have stomachs**;** they eat constantly.

Use a **comma** and a **coordinating conjunction** to make a compound sentence.

Sea horses don't have stomachs**,** **so** they eat constantly.

Read the sentence. Is it a run-on? Circle the answer.

1. Camels do not store water in their humps.   yes   no

2. Flamingos are pink their diet of shrimp and algae
   makes them that color.   yes   no

3. Toucans can curl into a ball they do this when they sleep.   yes   no

4. The smallest bones in the human body are in our ears.   yes   no

Read the run-on sentence. Then write a semicolon to correct it.

5. Each human has a unique smell it is as unique as a fingerprint.

6. You have no sense of smell when you sleep odors cannot disrupt sleep.

Science

Lab Experiments

You are doing experiments in your lab. Read the paragraph in the beaker. Then rewrite it in the other beaker so it has varied sentence patterns. You can add words or delete words.

Skills:
Vary sentence patterns;
Use specific theme-related words;
Produce sentences

You look through the microscope. You see a germ. You identify it. You mix a solution. It freezes the germ. You study the germ.

Find the science words. Circle them.
HINT Some may be backwards.

SCIENCE	SOLUTION	HYPOTHESIS
BEAKER	GERM	EXPERIMENT

R	Y	X	I	N	X	Y	S	G	R	M	E	P
S	R	D	S	O	P	P	C	A	N	R	S	R
Q	W	E	T	N	E	M	I	R	E	P	X	E
N	O	I	H	T	R	O	E	K	Q	X	M	K
S	O	L	U	T	I	O	N	Y	T	D	R	A
D	F	V	O	L	M	E	C	V	W	U	E	E
R	H	Y	P	O	T	H	E	S	I	S	G	B

Science

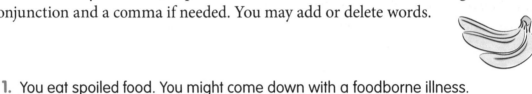

Write It Right!

Read each pair of sentences. Then rewrite the sentences as one complex sentence to vary the sentence pattern. Remember to use a subordinating conjunction and a comma if needed. You may add or delete words.

1. You eat spoiled food. You might come down with a foodborne illness.

    _____

    _____

2. The earliest humans had to eat what they could get. They ate a lot of fruit.

    _____

    _____

3. The first humans did not cook. They probably ate raw meat.

    _____

    _____

The sentences below are run-on sentences. Rewrite each run-on correctly as a compound sentence, a sentence with a semicolon, or two separate sentences.

4. Food scientists study food they study mainly the chemistry and biology of food.

    _____

    _____

5. Some food scientists study nutrition others focus on foods' chemical reactions.

    _____

    _____

Science

Skill Sharpeners: Grammar and Punctuation • EMC 9956 • © Evan-Moor Corp.

Ancient Science Language Run-ons

You are a scientist, and you have discovered an ancient written language of scientific symbols. Use the chart to translate the paragraph below. Write the paragraph in English, and use semicolons to correct the run-on sentences. Write commas and capital letters where they belong.

Ancient Science Language

know	the	where	water	drink	need	I
▲	●	■	★	■	↓	●
bring	to	safe	minerals	it	design	not
◆	◖	→	◆	◖	▲	★
is	system	do	villagers	tested	then	has
←	■	◖	●	◖	◆	◆
spring	far	will	located	a	carry	. ?
◖	■	●	↑	★	◖	| |

Science

Review

Skills:

Explain how to vary sentence patterns;

Explain what a run-on sentence is;

Explain three ways to correct a run-on sentence;

Write semicolons to correct run-on sentences;

Write sentences with varied sentence patterns

Science Helps Us

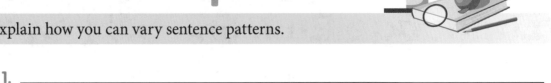

Explain how you can vary sentence patterns.

1. _____

_____

Explain what a run-on sentence is.

2. _____

_____

Write three sentences, each explaining a way to correct a run-on sentence.

3. _____

4. _____

5. _____

Read the run-on sentence. Then write a semicolon to correct it.

6. Scientists have changed the medical field, the food industry, and the way we care for our planet we are fortunate that scientists do the work they do.

7. Doctors, engineers, and other professionals use science in their jobs science is an important subject to learn.

Read the sentences. Then rewrite them as one sentence, and vary the sentence pattern. You can add words and delete words.

8. Scientists can study animals. Scientists can study our planet. Scientists can study the solar system.

_____

_____

Language Handbook

Grammar

Nouns

A **noun phrase** is a word or group of words that contains a noun or pronoun and all the words, phrases, or clauses that modify it.	a soldier the statue in Greece some cities **We** studied **the war**. **The book** describes **the battle in ancient Egypt**.

Verbs

An **verb phrase** is a word or group of words that contains a verb and includes all the words that relate to the action, including modifiers and objects.	writes types a paragraph seems cheerful Dorian **opened his backpack**. Yoko **runs to her classroom**.
A sentence must have **subject-verb agreement**. This means that a singular subject requires a singular verb, and a plural subject requires a plural verb.	**Singular subject and verb:** The <u>traveler</u> **buys** a train ticket. **Plural subject and verb:** The <u>travelers</u> **buy** train tickets.
An **inappropriate shift in verb tense** occurs when the verb tense in a sentence or paragraph changes without a reason.	**Inappropriate shift in verb tense:** The player **gets** the ball and **kicked** it. **Consistent verb tense:** The player **gets** the ball and **kicks** it.

Adjectives

A **proper adjective** is formed from a proper noun.	Hawaiian Chinese European American The **Korean** restaurant is closed today.

Adjectives *continued*

A **comparative adjective** compares more or less, usually between two nouns.	Shane's handwriting is **neater** than Anya's. I think math is **more difficult** than science.
A **superlative adjective** compares the most or least between three or more nouns.	My parents' bedroom is the **cleanest** room in the house. The dining room is the **most elegant** room of all.
Adjectives that appear together to modify the same noun and that provide different kinds of details go in a particular order. Read a sentence aloud to make sure the **order of adjectives** sounds correct.	This is the order of adjectives: **determiners, number, opinion, size, age, shape, color, origin, material, function** The two majestic massive young gray Indian elephants charged ahead quickly.

Pronouns

An **intensive pronoun** emphasizes the subject of a sentence by drawing attention to the person or thing doing the action.	myself yourself himself herself itself ourselves yourselves themselves Winona **herself** packed the suitcase.
A **vague pronoun** is a pronoun that does not have a clear antecedent or that has more than one possible antecedent.	The Smiths travel a lot. **It** is fun. The Smiths travel with their pets. **They** love going on trips. The Smiths and the Changs went on a trip. **Their** suitcases were heavy.
An **inappropriate shift in pronoun** occurs when pronouns that disagree in **number, gender,** or **point of view** are used to refer to a single antecedent.	She reads until **he** falls asleep. He or she reads until **they** fall asleep. They like to read until **you** fall asleep.

Prepositions

A **prepositional phrase** shows the relationship between a noun or pronoun and another word in a sentence. A preposition can describe location, time, or other kinds of relationships.

beside	in	through	of	between
before	for	with	at	about
behind	on	after	out	above

The children wait **for their dad**.

Mom is standing **beside the carousel**.

Sentences

A **compound sentence** has two independent clauses joined by a comma and a coordinating conjunction. There are **seven coordinating conjunctions**.

for	and	nor	but	or	yet	so

You have a ticket, **so** you can enter the fair.

I went on two rides, **but** I didn't buy any food.

A **complex sentence** has a dependent clause and an independent clause joined by a **subordinating conjunction**.

The dependent clause can be at the beginning or the end of the sentence.

before	unless	whenever	when	if
where	after	because	until	since

Whenever I eat cotton candy, I feel sick.

I feel sick **whenever** I eat cotton candy.

A **run-on sentence** occurs when two sentences are joined without correct punctuation.

Run-on sentence:

Janessa saw a statue it was from Greece.

Correct sentence:

Janessa saw a statue; it was from Greece.

Writing with **varied sentence patterns** has different kinds of sentences with different lengths, subjects, and word choices.

Dax rehearses his lines. How would he ever memorize them? He decided to make index cards, so he found the supplies. After making the cards, he asked Mom to help him rehearse.

Adverbs

An **adverb** describes how, when, or where an action happens.

genuinely   often   outdoors

Delia **clumsily** dropped her backpack.

Punctuation

Use a **comma** , to separate the day and the year in a date.	**May 20, 2022** **December 11, 2023** Seth's birthday party is on July 14, 2022.
Use a **comma** , to set off the year in a date from the rest of a sentence.	On April 18, 1906, there was a huge earthquake.
Use a **comma** , or commas to set off a nonessential appositive. An appositive is a noun phrase that renames a noun in the sentence. If you remove a nonessential appositive from the sentence, the sentence will still be complete and make sense.	Lakeesha got a new pet, a parakeet, last month. Pedro puts food, lettuce, into the bunny's bowl.
Use a **comma** , or commas to set off a nonrestrictive element, or a word, phrase, or clause that gives extra information that is not essential in a sentence. A nonrestrictive element can be removed from the sentence, and the sentence will still be complete.	Violet, who plays violin, will perform tonight. The band, marching, looks organized.
Use a **comma** , in a compound sentence before the coordinating conjunction that joins the two independent clauses.	I am ready to leave, but I need my coat. We got home, and we went right to bed.
Use a **comma** , in a complex sentence after the dependent clause when it is at the beginning of the sentence.	If he catches a fish, Junior will set it free. When he fishes, Dad uses plastic bait.
Use **commas** , to separate each item in a series.	You need peppers, onions, and tomatoes. Maria bought juice, milk, cereal, and tofu.
Use a **comma** , to set off an introductory element, or a word, phrase, or clause that comes before the main clause of the sentence.	Sweating, Valencia continued jogging. To cool himself down, Hunter drank cold water.

   Skill Sharpeners: Grammar and Punctuation • EMC 9956 • © Evan-Moor Corp.

Commas **,** continued

Use a **comma** **,** or commas to set off a quotation, or a speaker's words in a story.	"We'll leave early," Miranda said. "Yes," Freddy replied, "we can do that."
Use a **comma** **,** between coordinate adjectives. Coordinate adjectives appear together to provide details that are equally important.	Rico found an expensive, fancy hat at the store. Moshiri usually wears loose, baggy jeans.
Use a **comma** **,** and a coordinating conjunction to create a compound sentence to correct a **run-on sentence**.	**Run-on sentence:** There are raccoons in the yard they are huge. **Correct sentence:** There are raccoons in the yard, and they are huge.

Dashes **—**

Use a **dash** **—** or dashes to set off a nonrestrictive element.	Janie told her dad that her shoes — blue and white — had gotten wet.

Parentheses **( )**

Use a pair of **parentheses** **( )** to set off a nonrestrictive element.	My treehouse (which my dad built when I was little) is falling apart.

Colons **:**

Use a **colon** **:** after an independent clause to introduce an item or a list.	Betsy wants one thing for dinner: salad. Ebony wishes she wasn't allergic to these foods: nuts, honey, and eggs.

Semicolons ;

Use **semicolons** ; to separate items in a series when at least one item has a comma within it.	I saw Mrs. Turnpike, my teacher; Mr. Perez, my coach; and Dr. Sheldon, my dentist, at the fair.
Use a **semicolon** ; to separate two independent clauses to correct a **run-on sentence**.	Run-on sentence: Velma is in the school musical she has to memorize five songs. Correct sentence: Velma is in the school musical; she has to memorize five songs.

Titles of Books , Movies, and Television Shows

Underline titles of books, movies, and television shows.	Stewie used a recipe from <u>The International Cookbook for Kids</u> yesterday.

Quotation Marks " "

Use **quotation marks** " " around titles of songs, poems, articles, and short stories.	Sometimes I sing "My Girl" as I get ready for school in the morning.
Use **quotation marks** " " to show a speaker's exact words. Always use quotation marks in pairs.	"I don't want to cut the grass now!" said Peter. Felicia asked, "Can I do my chores later?"

Periods .

Use a **period** . and a capital letter to split up a **run-on sentence** and make it two separate sentences.	Run-on sentence: Mr. Valda washed his car his daughter helped him. Correct sentence: Mr. Valda washed his car. His daughter helped him.

Skill Sharpeners: Grammar and Punctuation • EMC 9956 • © Evan-Moor Corp.

Answer Key

Page 5

Grandpa's Trip Around the World

How many green noun phrases can you find in the story? **15**

How many orange commas can you find in the story? **8**

Page 6

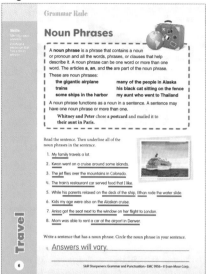

Noun Phrases

9. Answers will vary.

Page 7

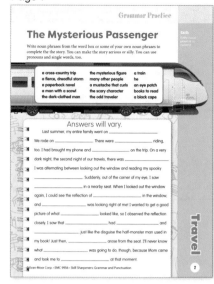

The Mysterious Passenger

Answers will vary.

Page 8

Commas with Dates

1. The last time I took a flight was on April 4, 2018.
2. The next cruise leaves on May 12, 2022, and goes up through Scandinavia.
3. The world's first commercial flight occurred on January 1, 1914.
4. Mom hasn't had to travel for work since September 29, 2018.
5. We picked up the rental car on November 18, 2018, and arrived on Thanksgiving.
6. August 4, 2017, was a special day for me because that's when we arrived in Hawaii.
7. I boarded the cruise ship on June 13, 2018, and sailed across the Atlantic.
8. Our train will depart on October 12, 2021, from Flagstaff, Arizona.
9. We should arrive in Stockholm on February 15, 2022.
10. Unfortunately, our flight for May 9, 2023, is cancelled.
11. Our cruise goes from October 28, 2024, to November 6, 2024.
12. March 11, 2021, will be the first day of our trip.
13. On April 14, 2018, we saw three whales alongside our ship.

Page 9

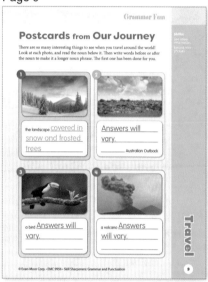

Postcards from Our Journey

1. the landscape covered in snow and frosted trees
2. Answers will vary. — Australian Outback
3. a bird Answers will vary.
4. a volcano Answers will vary.

Page 10

Write It Right!

1. Our train left the station in Chicago on February 9, 2016.
2. On June 8, 2022, our flight departs from the airport in Newark.
3. The Caribbean cruise went from December 20, 2017, until January 7, 2018.
4. On May 26, 2023, we will start our road trip by heading west.
5. It's been a tradition in our family since April 9, 2013, to visit Hawaii each year.
6. From October 19, 2022, until January 2, 2023, we will be in Europe.

Page 11

Come Fly Away!

1. There's a flight to Denver on July 5, 2021.
2. We fly from Rio de Janeiro to Lima on August 12, 2023.
3. We'll see you on October 10, 2020!
4. The plane lands on January 15, 2022.
5. January 18, 2024, is perfect for me.
6. Is March 25, 2021, okay?
7. November 20, 2022, is when we'll get together.
8. We're set to leave on May 21, 2017!
9. I think February 9, 2023, is when we'll take our flight.
10. Can you make it on August 6, 2024?
11. I'll arrive on March 14, 2021.
12. If September 8, 2022, doesn't work, we'll find another date.
13. We land on May 7, 2022, so we'll see you then.

1-A	2-B	3-C	4-D	5-E	6-F	7-G	8-H	9-I
10-J	11-K	12-L	13-M	14-N	15-O	16-P	17-Q	18-R
19-S	20-T	21-U	22-V	23-W	24-X	25-Y	26-Z	

E N J O Y Y O U R
5 14 1 15 25 25 15 21 18

F L I G H T
6 12 9 7 8 20

Page 12

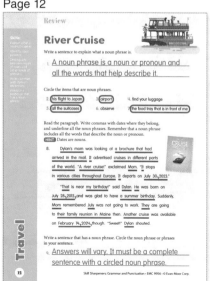

River Cruise

A noun phrase is a noun or pronoun and all the words that help describe it.

Circle the items that are noun phrases.
- his flight to Japan
- airport
- find your luggage
- all the suitcases
- observe
- the food tray that is in front of me

9. Answers will vary. It must be a complete sentence with a circled noun phrase.

Page 13

Green Horizon

How many green verb phrases can you find in the story? **13**

How many orange commas can you find in the story? **9**

Page 14

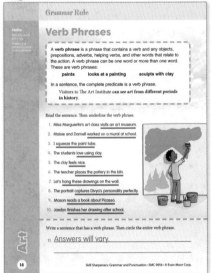

Verb Phrases

A **verb phrase** is a phrase that contains a verb and any objects, prepositions, adverbs, helping verbs, and other words that relate to the action. A verb phrase can be one word or more than one word. These are verb phrases:

paints   looks at a painting   sculpts with clay

In a sentence, the complete predicate is a verb phrase.

Visitors to The Art Institute **can see art from different periods in history.**

Read the sentence. Then underline the verb phrase.

1. Miss Marguerite's art class visits an art museum.
2. Maisie and Darnell worked on a mural at school.
3. I squeeze the paint tube.
4. The students love using clay.
5. The clay feels nice.
6. The teacher places the pottery in the kiln.
7. Let's hang these drawings on the wall.
8. The portrait captures Divya's personality perfectly.
9. Mason reads a book about Picasso.
10. Jaedyn finishes her drawing after school.

Write a sentence that has a verb phrase. Then circle the entire verb phrase.

11. Answers will vary.

Page 15

Still Life

A verb phrase may use an **action verb** or a **linking verb**. Read the sentence, and underline the verb phrase. Then write *action* or *linking* to describe the verb in the phrase.

1. Mr. Gilberto places items on a table. — action
2. The items look interesting. — linking
3. Zeke paints slowly. — action
4. Roxy creates a glass bottle with the paint. — action
5. Mohammad washes his paintbrush. — action
6. Dylan is talented. — linking
7. The students make nice drawings. — action
8. Some objects are difficult to paint. — linking
9. Nathan's paintbrush glides across the canvas. — action
10. Zoe becomes quiet. — linking
11. She concentrates on her painting. — action
12. Mr. Gilberto advises Fritz. — action
13. The teacher seems happy with the students' work. — linking
14. Sam is done with her painting. — linking
15. Everyone admires one another's amazing work. — action

Write a sentence with a verb phrase that uses a linking verb.

16. Answers will vary.

Page 16

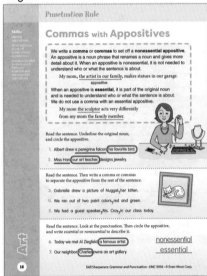

Commas with Appositives

We write a **comma** or **commas** to set off a **nonessential appositive**. An appositive is a noun phrase that renames a noun and gives more detail about it. When an appositive is nonessential, it is not needed to understand who or what the sentence is about.

My mom, the artist in our family, makes statues in our garage.
appositive

When an appositive is **essential**, it is part of the original noun and is needed to understand who or what the sentence is about. We do not use a comma with an essential appositive.

My mom the sculptor acts very differently from my mom the family member.

Read the sentence. Underline the original noun, and circle the appositive.

1. Albert drew a peregrine falcon, his favorite bird.
2. Miss Han, our art teacher, designs jewelry.

Read the sentence. Then write a comma or commas to separate the appositive from the rest of the sentence.

3. Gabrielle drew a picture of Nugget, her kitten.
4. We ran out of two paint colors, red and green.
5. We had a guest speaker, Ms. Croy, in our class today.

Read the sentence. Look at the punctuation. Then circle the appositive, and write *essential* or *nonessential* to describe it.

6. Today we met Al Ziegfeld, a famous artist. — nonessential
7. Our neighbor Charles owns an art gallery. — essential

Page 17

Photographs Tell a Story

Look at the photograph, and read the subject of the sentence. Then complete the sentence by writing a verb phrase that says what you see in the photograph.
Examples are shown.

1. The girl takes a selfie
2. This family spends time at the beach
3. An elephant sits on a log
4. These boys sing songs

Read the verb phrase below. Draw a picture of a subject doing what the verb phrase describes.

paints a family portrait — Answers will vary.

Page 18

Write It Right!

The sentences below have misplaced verb phrases and comma errors with appositives. Some sentences have missing or misplaced commas or commas that are not needed. Read the sentences carefully. Then write them correctly.

1. Ava my friend is a very talented artist.
Ava, my friend, is a very talented artist.

2. My, Aunt, Kemala a sculpting demonstration did for my class.
My Aunt Kemala did a sculpting demonstration for my class.

3. Fills an entire wall our class mural the one with the rainforest.
Our class mural, the one with the rainforest, fills an entire wall.

4. Painted a picture of me and all my other brothers my brother Marco.
My brother Marco painted a picture of me and all my other brothers.

5. Looks better than my red, painting my latest painting the blue one.
My latest painting, the blue one, looks better than my red painting.

6. Mr. Vernassi my art teacher says art can be healing.
Mr. Vernassi, my art teacher, says art can be healing.

Page 19

Appositive Bingo!

Read the sentences on the bingo card. Color the squares that have sentences with correct punctuation.

BONUS Now write commas where they belong on the squares you did not color on the bingo card.

Page 20

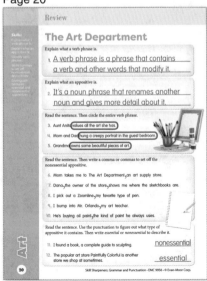

The Art Department

Explain what a verb phrase is.

1. A verb phrase is a phrase that contains a verb and other words that modify it.

Explain what an appositive is.

2. It's a noun phrase that renames another noun and gives more detail about it.

Read the sentence. Then circle the entire verb phrase.

3. Aunt Anita values all the art she has.
4. Mom and Dad hung a creepy portrait in the guest bedroom.
5. Grandma owns some beautiful pieces of art.

Read the sentence. Then write a comma or commas to set off the nonessential appositive.

6. Mom takes me to The Art Department, an art supply store.
7. Dana, the owner of the store, shows me where the sketchbooks are.
8. I pick out a Zoomline, my favorite type of pen.
9. I bump into Mr. Orlando, my art teacher.
10. He's buying oil paint, the kind of paint he always uses.

Read the sentence. Use the punctuation to figure out what type of appositive it contains. Then write *essential* or *nonessential* to describe it.

11. I found a book, a complete guide to sculpting. — nonessential
12. The popular art store Paintfully Colorful is another store we shop at sometimes. — essential

Page 21

Story

Read the text.

A Collection of City-States

Long before Greece was a country, it was a collection of city-states. Greek city-states, which had their own laws and armies, were quite distinct from one another. Sparta, which was ruled by warriors, had a fearsome army. Spartan boys, who began training at the age of seven, had to join the military. The city-state of Corinth invested in public works projects, which kept their citizens busy working. Corinthian citizens enjoyed luxuries such as bathhouses, or buildings with baths for the public. Argos, made up of multiple places, was a long-time rival of Sparta. Argive citizens became renowned traders. Megara, located on the coast, granted its citizens a lot of freedom. Megarian sailors traveled seamlessly throughout the Mediterranean Sea. The greatest of the city-states was Athens, named for the goddess Athena. Athenian schools were considered the best of all the city-states' schools. Culture and the arts thrived in Athens. It was also the birthplace of democracy. As you can see, each city-state made a unique contribution to Greek civilization.

Read the rules. Answer the questions.

Grammar Proper adjectives, such as the names of geographic places, are formed from proper nouns. Proper adjectives are capitalized.

How many proper adjectives can you find in the text? — 6

Punctuation We write a comma , or commas to set off nonrestrictive elements, or words, phrases, or clauses that give extra information that is not essential in a sentence.

How many purple commas can you find in the text? — 13

Page 22

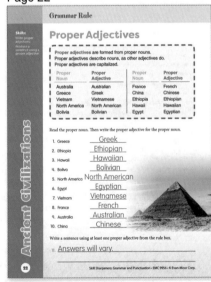

Proper Adjectives

Proper adjectives are formed from proper nouns. Proper adjectives describe nouns, as other adjectives do. Proper adjectives are capitalized.

Proper Noun	Proper Adjective	Proper Noun	Proper Adjective
Australia	Australian	France	French
Greece	Greek	China	Chinese
Vietnam	Vietnamese	Ethiopia	Ethiopian
North America	North American	Hawaii	Hawaiian
Bolivia	Bolivian	Egypt	Egyptian

Read the proper noun. Then write the proper adjective for the proper noun.

1. Greece — Greek
2. Ethiopia — Ethiopian
3. Hawaii — Hawaiian
4. Bolivia — Bolivian
5. North America — North American
6. Egypt — Egyptian
7. Vietnam — Vietnamese
8. France — French
9. Australia — Australian
10. China — Chinese

Write a sentence using at least one proper adjective from the rule box.

11. Answers will vary.

Page 23

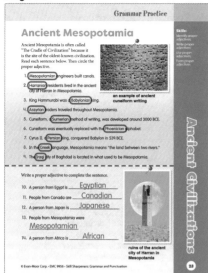

Grammar Practice

Ancient Mesopotamia

Ancient Mesopotamia is often called "The Cradle of Civilization" because it is the site of the oldest-known civilization. Read each sentence below. Then circle the proper adjective.

1. (Mesopotamian) engineers built canals.
2. (Harranian) residents lived in the ancient city of Harran in Mesopotamia.
3. King Hammurabi was a (Babylonian) king.
4. (Assyrian) traders traveled throughout Mesopotamia.
5. Cuneiform, a (Sumerian) method of writing, was developed around 3000 BCE.
6. Cuneiform was eventually replaced with the (Phoenician) alphabet.
7. Cyrus II, a (Persian) king, conquered Babylon in 539 BCE.
8. In the (Greek) language, Mesopotamia means "the land between two rivers."
9. The (Iraqi) city of Baghdad is located in what used to be Mesopotamia.

Write a proper adjective to complete the sentence.

10. A person from Egypt is __Egyptian__.
11. People from Canada are __Canadian__.
12. A person from Japan is __Japanese__.
13. People from Mesopotamia were __Mesopotamian__.
14. A person from Africa is __African__.

an example of ancient cuneiform writing

ruins of the ancient city of Harran in Mesopotamia

Ancient Civilizations

Page 24

Punctuation Rule

Commas with Nonrestrictive Elements

statue of Emperor Augustus

We write a **comma** or **commas** to set off a nonrestrictive element in a sentence. A nonrestrictive element is a word, phrase, or clause that gives extra information about a subject in the sentence. If a nonrestrictive element were removed from the sentence, the sentence would still be complete and make sense.

nonrestrictive element
Archaeologists found one type of object, toys, in abundance when excavating the area where the Indus River valley civilization had been.

nonrestrictive element
The Saraswati River, which the Indus River valley civilization depended on, is believed to have dried up thousands of years ago.

Read the sentence. Is the nonrestrictive element punctuated correctly? Write *yes* or *no*.

1. Augustus, who was the son of Julius Caesar, was the first Roman emperor. __yes__
2. The Aztecs who settled in Mexico in the 1300s were originally nomadic. __no__
3. Romans raced chariots in the Circus Maximus arena one of the largest sports arenas ever built. __no__
4. King Tutankhamun an Egyptian pharaoh died at the age of 19. __no__

Read the sentence. Then write a comma or commas to set off the nonrestrictive element.

5. The Nile delta, which leads to the sea, allowed Egyptians to trade with Europe.
6. Montezuma, an Aztec leader, expanded the empire.

Ancient Civilizations

Page 25

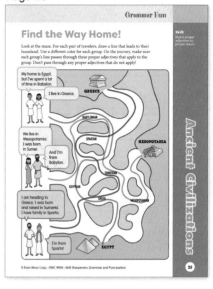

Grammar Fun

Find the Way Home!

Look at the maze. For each pair of travelers, draw a line that leads to their homeland. Use a different color for each group. On the journey, make sure each group's line passes through three proper adjectives that apply to the group. Don't pass through any proper adjectives that do not apply!

My home is Egypt, but I've spent a lot of time in Babylon.

I live in Greece.

We live in Mesopotamia. I was born in Sumer.

And I'm from Babylon.

I am heading to Greece. I was born and raised in Sumeria. I have family in Sparta.

I'm from Sparta!

Ancient Civilizations

Page 26

Application

Write It Right!

a ziggurat

The sentences below have proper adjective errors and punctuation errors with nonrestrictive elements. Read the sentences carefully. Then write them correctly.

1. The Sphinx an ancient egyptian statue sits in Giza, Egypt.
   __The Sphinx, an ancient Egyptian statue, sits in Giza, Egypt.__
2. At the center of every sumerian city was a ziggurat used for religious activities.
   __At the center of every Sumerian city was a ziggurat, used for religious activities.__
3. Silk which is a type of fabric fascinated many members of roman society.
   __Silk, which is a type of fabric, fascinated many members of Roman society.__
4. Persepolis surrounded by a 30-foot wall was built in terraces.
   __Persepolis, surrounded by a 30-foot wall, was built in terraces.__
5. The Indus River valley civilization was also known as the harappan civilization.
   __The Indus River valley civilization was also known as the Harappan civilization.__
6. Hieroglyphics a writing system was used by ancient egyptian people.
   __Hieroglyphics, a writing system, was used by ancient Egyptian people.__

Ancient Civilizations

Page 27

Punctuation Fun

Sentence Spirals

Each spiral describes an ancient civilization. Read the sentences in each spiral, and write commas to set off the nonrestrictive elements. Then write the letter that comes directly after each comma you wrote in the spiral. After you write the letters, unscramble them to find out the name of the country where the ancient civilization was located. Write the country's name on the line.

China

Egypt

Greece

Ancient Civilizations

Page 28

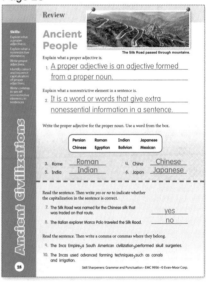

Review

Ancient People

The Silk Road passed through mountains.

Explain what a proper adjective is.
1. __A proper adjective is an adjective formed from a proper noun.__

Explain what a nonrestrictive element in a sentence is.
2. __It is a word or words that give extra nonessential information in a sentence.__

Write the proper adjective for the proper noun. Use a word from the box.

Persian	Roman	Indian	Japanese
Chinese	Egyptian	Bolivian	Mexican

3. Rome __Roman__ 4. China __Chinese__
5. India __Indian__ 6. Japan __Japanese__

Read the sentence. Then write *yes* or *no* to indicate whether the capitalization in the sentence is correct.

7. The Silk Road was named for the Chinese silk that was traded on that route. __yes__
8. The Italian explorer Marco Polo traveled the Silk Road. __no__

Read the sentence. Then write a comma or commas where they belong.

9. The Inca Empire, a South American civilization, performed skull surgeries.
10. The Incas used advanced farming techniques, such as canals and irrigation.

Ancient Civilizations

Page 29

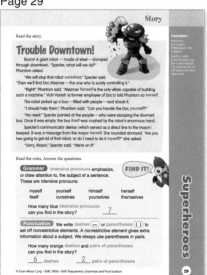

Story

Trouble Downtown!

Read the story.

Boom! A giant robot—made of steel—stomped through downtown. "Specter, what will we do?" Phantom asked.

"We will stop that robot ourselves," Specter said.
"Then we'll find Doc Mezmer—the one who is surely controlling it."

"Right!" Phantom said. "Mezmer himself is the only villain capable of building such a machine." Vicki Vanish, a former employee of Doc's, told Phantom so herself.

The robot picked up a bus—filled with people—and shook it.

"I should help them," Phantom said. "Can you handle the Doc yourself?"

"No need." Specter pointed at the people—who were escaping the doomed bus. Once it was empty, the bus itself was crushed by the robot's enormous hand.

Specter's communicator device (which served as a direct line to the mayor) beeped. It was a message from the mayor herself. "Are you two going to get rid of that robot, or do I need to do it myself?" she asked.

"Sorry, Mayor," Specter said. "We're on it!"

Read the rules. Answer the questions.

Grammar Intensive pronouns emphasize, or draw attention to, the subject of a sentence. These are intensive pronouns:

myself   yourself   himself   herself
itself   ourselves   yourselves   themselves

How many intensive pronouns can you find in the story? __7__

Punctuation We write dashes (—) or parentheses ( ) to set off nonrestrictive elements. A nonrestrictive element gives extra information about a subject. We always use parentheses in pairs.

How many orange dashes and pairs of parentheses can you find in the story?
__5__ dashes   __2__ pairs of parentheses

Superheroes

Page 30

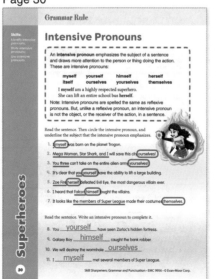

Grammar Rule

Intensive Pronouns

An **intensive pronoun** emphasizes the subject of a sentence and draws more attention to the person or thing doing the action. These are intensive pronouns:

myself   yourself   himself   herself
itself   ourselves   yourselves   themselves

I myself am a highly respected superhero.
She can lift an entire school bus herself.

Note: Intensive pronouns sound the same as reflexive pronouns. But, unlike a reflexive pronoun, an intensive pronoun is not the object, or the receiver of the action, in a sentence.

Read the sentence. Then circle the intensive pronoun, and underline the subject that the intensive pronoun emphasizes.

1. I myself was born on the planet Trogon.
2. Mega Woman, Star Shark, and I will save this city ourselves!
3. You three can't take on the entire alien army yourselves!
4. It's clear that you yourself have the ability to lift a large building.
5. Zoe Fire herself defeated Evil Eye, the most dangerous villain ever.
6. I heard that Falcon himself fought the villains.
7. It looks like the members of Super League made their costumes themselves.

Read the sentence. Write an intensive pronoun to complete it.

8. You __yourself__ have seen Zorloc's hidden fortress.
9. Galaxy Boy __himself__ caught the bank robber.
10. We will destroy the wormhole __ourselves__.
11. I __myself__ met several members of Super League.

Superheroes

Page 31

Grammar Practice

The New Recruit

Read the story. Then write intensive pronouns for the underlined subjects. The first one has been done for you.

1. Team Ultra recruited me, Starkid, last week.

You see, I __myself__ have the ability to sense danger before it happens. Samantha Storm called me __herself__ and said, "Starkid, we here at Team Ultra protect the world. But we can't always do it __ourselves__. You __yourself__ foiled Dino Punk's plan to build the mega-ray. How about joining us?"

I went to the Team Ultra headquarters. The building __itself__ doesn't look like much from the outside. Inside, however, I saw amazing technology. Mac Brainwave designed the technology __himself__.

Suddenly, I had a superhero vision. "Alien invaders are about to attack Earth!" I exclaimed.

"Impossible!" Mac said. "My equipment isn't picking up any signal."

"They're coming through a wormhole," I said. "They built it __themselves__." The team followed up on my superhero information, and it turned out that I was right. I even helped the team prevent the aliens from invading. Afterward, I was part of Team Ultra!

Write a sentence using an intensive pronoun.
2. __Answers will vary.__

Superheroes

To download a larger version of this answer key, go to: ***www.evan-moor.com/resources***
Enter your email address and this resource code: **EMC9956**

Page 32

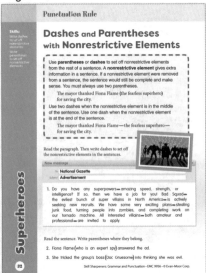

Punctuation Rule

Dashes and Parentheses with Nonrestrictive Elements

Use **parentheses** or **dashes** to set off nonrestrictive elements from the rest of a sentence. A **nonrestrictive element** gives extra information in a sentence. If a nonrestrictive element were removed from a sentence, the sentence would still be complete and make sense. You must always use two parentheses.

The mayor thanked Fiona Flame (the fearless superhero) for saving the city.

Use two dashes when the nonrestrictive element is in the middle of the sentence. Use one dash when the nonrestrictive element is at the end of the sentence.

The mayor thanked Fiona Flame—the fearless superhero—for saving the city.

Read the paragraph. Then write dashes to set off the nonrestrictive elements in the sentences.

New message
To: National Gazette
Subject: Advertisement

1. Do you have any superpowers—amazing speed, strength, or intelligence? If so, then we have a job for you! Bad Squad—the evilest bunch of super villains in North America—is actively seeking new recruits. We have some very exciting plans—stealing junk food, turning people into zombies, and completing work on our tornado machine. All interested villains—both amateur and professional—are invited to apply.

Read the sentence. Write parentheses where they belong.

2. Fiona Flame (who is an expert spy) answered the ad.
3. She tricked the group's boss (Doc Gruesome) into thinking she was evil.

Superheroes

32 Skill Sharpeners: Grammar and Punctuation • EMC 9956 • © Evan-Moor Corp.

Page 33

Grammar Fun

Heroes and Villains

Look at the pictures of the superheroes and villains. Read the description of each superhero. Then write an intensive pronoun in the sentence. Last, unscramble the bold letters to form the villain's name and complete the sentence.

1. Bolt Girl herself defeated the f u r m a n plus many others.
2. His powerful super cape can fight villains such as i c e p a i n all by itself.
3. We ourselves harness great powers to beat the villain g h o s t.
4. You yourself must ruin the evil plans of i n s e c t m a n so he can't win.
5. Athletic Man himself won against c l a w.
6. I myself effortlessly extinguished the blaze of my enemy, f l a m e.

Superheroes

© Evan-Moor Corp. • EMC 9956 • Skill Sharpeners: Grammar and Punctuation 33

Page 34

Application

Write It Right!

The following sentences have intensive pronoun errors and punctuation errors with nonrestrictive elements. Read the sentences carefully. Then rewrite the sentences correctly, adding dashes to set off the nonrestrictive elements.

1. My supercar which can fly and go underwater uses the newest technology.
My supercar—which can fly and go underwater—uses the newest technology.
2. Zelgor itself is a clumsy villain his mistakes being well known by all.
Zelgor himself is a clumsy villain—his mistakes being well known by all.
3. She himself found what she was looking for the villain's hideout.
She herself found what she was looking for—the villain's hideout.

The following sentences have intensive pronoun errors and punctuation errors with nonrestrictive elements. Read the sentences carefully. Then rewrite the sentences correctly, using parentheses where they belong.
HINT End punctuation goes outside the parentheses.

4. Unfortunately, I yourself couldn't defeat Troga the enormous turtle monster.
Unfortunately, I myself couldn't defeat Troga (the enormous turtle monster).
5. You myself must stop Volt by tonight which is when he will shrink the city.
Your yourself must stop Volt by tonight (which is when he will shrink the city).

Superheroes

34 Skill Sharpeners: Grammar and Punctuation • EMC 9956 • © Evan-Moor Corp.

Page 35

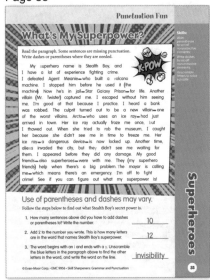

Punctuation Fun

What's My Superpower?

Read the paragraph. Some sentences are missing punctuation. Write dashes or parentheses where they are needed.

My superhero name is Stealth Boy, and I have a lot of experience fighting crime. I defeated Agent Meanie—who built a volcano machine. I stopped him before he used it (the machine). Now he's in jail—Star Galaxy Prison—for life. Another villain (Mr. Twister) captured me. I escaped without him seeing me. I'm good at that because I practice. I heard a bank was robbed. The culprit turned out to be a new villain—one of the worst villains. Arcto—who uses an ice ray—had just arrived in town. Her ice ray actually froze me once, but I thawed out. When she tried to rob the museum, I caught her because she didn't see me in time to freeze me. Her ice ray—a dangerous device—is now locked up. Another time, aliens invaded the city, but they didn't see me waiting for them. I appeared before they did any damage. My good friends—also superheroes—were with me. They (my superhero friends) help when there's a big problem. The mayor is calling me—which means there's an emergency. I'm off to fight crime! See if you can figure out what my superpower is!

Use of parentheses and dashes may vary.

Follow the steps below to find out what Stealth Boy's secret power is.

1. How many sentences above did you have to add dashes or parentheses to? Write the number. 10
2. Add 2 to the number you wrote. This is how many letters are in the word that names Stealth Boy's superpower. 12
3. The word begins with an i and ends with a y. Unscramble the blue letters in the paragraph above to find the other letters in the word, and write the word on the line. invisibility

Superheroes

© Evan-Moor Corp. • EMC 9956 • Skill Sharpeners: Grammar and Punctuation 35

Page 36

Review

Helio to the Rescue!

Explain what an intensive pronoun is.

1. An intensive pronoun is a pronoun that emphasizes a subject and draws more attention to it.

Write the eight intensive pronouns.

2. myself yourself himself herself itself ourselves yourselves themselves

Explain how you can use parentheses and dashes in a sentence.

3. You can use parentheses or dashes to set off a nonrestrictive element from the rest of a sentence.

Write a sentence with an intensive pronoun.

4. Answers will vary.

Read the sentence. Write parentheses where they belong.

5. Helio (who uses the energy of stars) can travel anywhere in the universe.
6. The space-traveling hero drifts by his home planet (called Omega 360).

Read the sentence. Write a dash or dashes where they belong.

7. Helio receives a distress call from Team Ultra—a superhero team from Earth.
8. The members of Team Ultra—in desperate need of help—cheer when Helio arrives!

Superheroes

36 Skill Sharpeners: Grammar and Punctuation • EMC 9956 • © Evan-Moor Corp.

Page 37

Story

Read the story.

The New Tent

Last weekend, my family headed to the forest for our favorite activity: camping! We picked a spot beside a lake. It was the perfect spot: peaceful, scenic, and comfortable. The ground was level, and there was diversity in the terrain: water, trees, and hills. The leaves above us provided shade, and we still had cellphone service, in case of an emergency. After picking the campsite, the next thing we had to do was obvious: set up camp! Mom and I grabbed supplies from the car while Manuel got to work on our new tent. I placed camp chairs around the fire pit, and Mom put the cooking gear on the picnic table. Manuel, meanwhile, was struggling with the tent. I helped Dad gather wood for a fire. Dad and Mom got a fire going and started cooking. And Manuel was still struggling with the tent! Various parts of the tent were strewn across the ground. By this time, Manuel was grunting and frustrated. At that point, Dad asked Manuel one question: "Do you need help?" Working together, they finally got the tent set up. As we all ate, Manuel laughed and joked about how he'd almost lost his taste for camping because of a tent!

Read the rules. Answer the questions.

Grammar A prepositional phrase shows the relationship between a noun or pronoun and another word in a sentence. Prepositional phrases can describe location, time, and other kinds of relationships.

FIND IT!

How many green prepositional phrases can you find in the story? 11

Punctuation We write a colon (:) after an independent clause to introduce an item or a list.

How many orange colons can you find in the story? 5

The Great Outdoors

© Evan-Moor Corp. • EMC 9956 • Skill Sharpeners: Grammar and Punctuation 37

Page 38

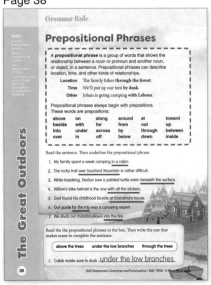

Grammar Rule

Prepositional Phrases

A **prepositional phrase** is a group of words that shows the relationship between a noun or pronoun and another noun, or object, in a sentence. Prepositional phrases can describe location, time, and other kinds of relationships.

Location	The family hikes **through the forest**.
Time	We'll put up our tent **by dusk**.
Other	Johan is going camping **with Lebron**.

Prepositional phrases always begin with prepositions. These words are prepositions:

above	on	along	around	at	toward
beside	with	for	from	out	up
into	under	across	by	through	between
over	in	off	below	down	inside

Read the sentence. Then underline the prepositional phrase.

1. My family spent a week camping in a cabin.
2. The rocky trail over Sourland Mountain is rather difficult.
3. While kayaking, Declan saw a painted turtle swim beneath the surface.
4. Willow's bike helmet is the one with all the stickers.
5. Dad found his childhood bicycle at Grandma's house.
6. Our guide for the trip was a canoeing expert.
7. We stuck our marshmallows into the fire.

Read the the prepositional phrases in the box. Then write the one that makes sense to complete the sentence.

above the trees | under the low branches | through the trees

8. Caleb made sure to duck under the low branches.

The Great Outdoors

38 Skill Sharpeners: Grammar and Punctuation • EMC 9956 • © Evan-Moor Corp.

Page 39

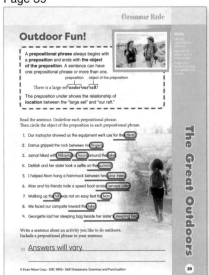

Grammar Rule

Outdoor Fun!

A **prepositional phrase** always begins with **a preposition** and ends with **the object of the preposition**. A sentence can have one prepositional phrase or more than one.

There is a large eel **under our raft**. (preposition: under; object of the preposition: raft)

The preposition *under* shows the relationship of **location** between the "large eel" and "our raft."

Read the sentence. Underline each prepositional phrase. Then circle the object of the preposition in each prepositional phrase.

1. Our instructor showed us the equipment we'll use for the climb.
2. Darius gripped the rock between his fingers.
3. Jamal hiked with Mikayla for hours around the lake.
4. Delilah and her sister took a selfie on the summit.
5. I helped Mom hang a hammock between two pine trees.
6. Max and his friends rode a speed boat across Lenape Lake.
7. Walking up the hill was not an easy feat for Ivan.
8. We faced our campsite toward the lake.
9. Georgette laid her sleeping bag beside her sister's sleeping bag.

Write a sentence about an activity you like to do outdoors. Include a prepositional phrase in your sentence.

10. Answers will vary.

The Great Outdoors

© Evan-Moor Corp. • EMC 9956 • Skill Sharpeners: Grammar and Punctuation 39

Page 40

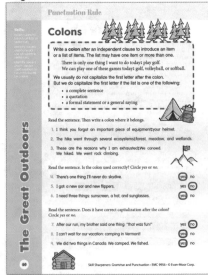

Punctuation Rule

Colons

Write a **colon** after an independent clause to introduce an item or a list of items. The list may have one item or more than one.

There is only one thing I want to do today: play golf.
We can play one of these games today: golf, volleyball, or softball.

We usually do not capitalize the first letter after the colon. But we do capitalize the first letter if the list is one of the following:

- a complete sentence
- a quotation
- a formal statement or a general saying

Read the sentence. Then write a colon where it belongs.

1. I think you forgot an important piece of equipment: your helmet.
2. The hike went through several ecosystems: forest, meadow, and wetlands.
3. These are the reasons why I am exhausted: We canoed. We hiked. We went rock climbing.

Read the sentence. Is the colon used correctly? Circle *yes* or *no*.

4. There's one thing I'll never do: skydive. (yes) no
5. I got: a new oar and new flippers. yes (no)
6. I need three things: sunscreen, a hat, and sunglasses. (yes) no

Read the sentence. Does it have correct capitalization after the colon? Circle *yes* or *no*.

7. After our run, my brother said one thing: "that was fun!" yes (no)
8. I can't wait for our vacation: camping in Vermont! (yes) no
9. We did two things in Canada: We camped. We fished. (yes) no

The Great Outdoors

40 Skill Sharpeners: Grammar and Punctuation • EMC 9956 • © Evan-Moor Corp.

Page 41

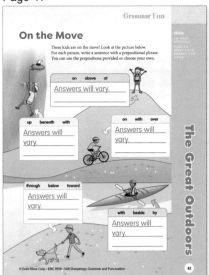

On the Move

These kids are on the move! Look at the picture below.
For each person, write a sentence with a prepositional phrase.
You can use the prepositions provided or choose your own.

on · above · at
Answers will vary.

up · beneath · with
Answers will vary.

on · with · over
Answers will vary.

through · below · toward
Answers will vary.

with · beside · by
Answers will vary.

The Great Outdoors

Page 42

Write It Right!

The sentences below have misplaced prepositions and colon errors. Read the sentences carefully. Then write them correctly.

1. The trails the mountain are tough on.
   The trails on the mountain are tough.

2. We have everything we need paddles, vests, and canoes.
   We have everything we need: paddles, vests, and canoes.

3. "This is a long hike," Keisha said a tired voice with.
   "This is a long hike," Keisha said with a tired voice.

4. There were lots of obstacles the trail on roots, rocks, and a log.
   There were lots of obstacles on the trail: roots, rocks, and a log.

5. Marie was being silly when she tried to row the river up!
   Marie was being silly when she tried to row up the river!

6. Jake wants: to do three things He wants to swim. He wants to climb. He wants to fish.
   Jake wants to do three things: He wants to swim. He wants to climb. He wants to fish.

The Great Outdoors

Page 43

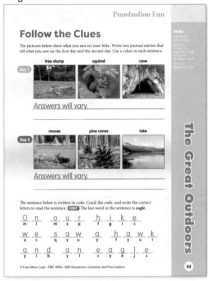

Follow the Clues

The pictures below show what you saw on your hike. Write two journal entries that tell what you saw on the first day and the second day. Use a colon in each sentence.

Day 1 — tree stump · squirrel · cave
Answers will vary.

Day 2 — moose · pine cones · lake
Answers will vary.

The sentence below is written in code. Crack the code, and write the correct letters to read the sentence. **HINT** The last word in the sentence is **eagle**.

On our hike
we saw a hawk
and an eagle

The Great Outdoors

Page 44

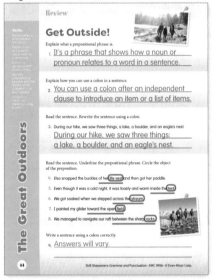

Get Outside!

Explain what a prepositional phrase is.

1. It's a phrase that shows how a noun or pronoun relates to a word in a sentence.

Explain how you can use a colon in a sentence.

2. You can use a colon after an independent clause to introduce an item or a list of items.

Read the sentence. Rewrite the sentence using a colon.

3. During our hike, we saw three things, a lake, a boulder, and an eagle's nest.
   During our hike, we saw three things: a lake, a boulder, and an eagle's nest.

Read the sentence. Underline the prepositional phrase. Circle the object of the preposition.

4. Elsa snapped the buckles of her life vest and then got her paddle.
5. Even though it was a cold night, it was toasty and warm inside the tent.
6. We got soaked when we stepped across the stream.
7. I pointed my glider toward the open field.
8. We managed to navigate our raft between the sharp rocks.

Write a sentence using a colon correctly.

9. Answers will vary.

The Great Outdoors

Page 45

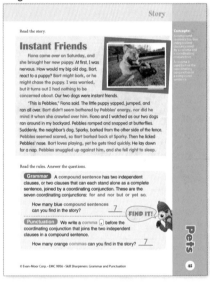

Instant Friends

Read the story.

Fiona came over on Saturday, and she brought her new puppy. At first, I was nervous. How would my old dog, Bart, react to a puppy? Bart might bark, or he might chase the puppy. I was worried, but it turns out I had nothing to be concerned about. Our two dogs were instant friends.

"This is Pebbles," Fiona said. The little puppy yapped, jumped, and ran all over. Bart didn't seem bothered by Pebbles' energy, nor did he mind it when she crawled over him. Fiona and I watched as our two dogs ran around in my backyard. Pebbles romped and snapped at butterflies. Suddenly, the neighbor's dog, Sparky, barked from the other side of the fence. Pebbles seemed scared, so Bart barked back at Sparky. Then he licked Pebbles' nose. Bart loves playing, yet he gets tired quickly. He lay down for a nap. Pebbles snuggled up against him, and she fell right to sleep.

Read the rules. Answer the questions.

Grammar A compound sentence has two independent clauses, or two clauses that can each stand alone as a complete sentence, joined by a coordinating conjunction. These are the seven coordinating conjunctions: for and nor but or yet so.

How many blue compound sentences can you find in the story?   7   **FIND IT!**

Punctuation We write a comma (,) before the coordinating conjunction that joins the two independent clauses in a compound sentence.

How many orange commas can you find in the story?   7

Pets

Page 46

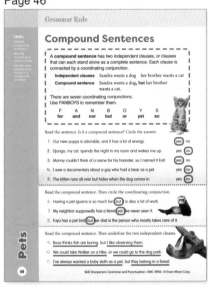

Compound Sentences

A **compound sentence** has two independent clauses, or clauses that can each stand alone as a complete sentence. Each clause is connected by a coordinating conjunction.

Independent clauses   Sandra wants a dog   her brother wants a cat
Compound sentence   Sandra wants a dog, but her brother wants a cat.

There are seven coordinating conjunctions.
Use FANBOYS to remember them.

F — for   A — and   N — nor   B — but   O — or   Y — yet   S — so

Read the sentence. Is it a compound sentence? Circle the answer.

1. Our new puppy is adorable, and it has a lot of energy.   **yes**   no
2. Django, my cat, spends the night in my room and wakes me up.   yes   **no**
3. Manny couldn't think of a name for his hamster, so I named it Earl.   **yes**   no
4. I saw a documentary about a guy who had a bear as a pet.   yes   **no**
5. The kitten runs all over but hides when the dog comes in.   yes   **no**

Read the compound sentence. Then circle the coordinating conjunction.

6. Having a pet iguana is so much fun, but it also a lot of work.
7. My neighbor supposedly has a ferret, yet I've never seen it.
8. Fuyu has a pet bird, but her dad is the person who mostly takes care of it.

Read the compound sentence. Then underline the two independent clauses.

9. Rosa thinks fish are boring, but I like observing them.
10. We could take Walker on a hike, or we could go to the dog park.
11. I've always wanted a baby sloth as a pet, but they belong in a forest.

Pets

Page 47

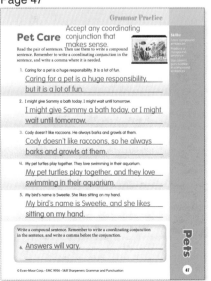

Pet Care   Accept any coordinating conjunction that makes sense.

Read the pair of sentences. Then use them to write a compound sentence. Remember to write a coordinating conjunction in the sentence, and write a comma where it is needed.

1. Caring for a pet is a huge responsibility. It is a lot of fun.
   Caring for a pet is a huge responsibility, but it is a lot of fun.

2. I might give Sammy a bath today. I might wait until tomorrow.
   I might give Sammy a bath today, or I might wait until tomorrow.

3. Cody doesn't like raccoons. He always barks and growls at them.
   Cody doesn't like raccoons, so he always barks and growls at them.

4. My pet turtles play together. They love swimming in their aquarium.
   My pet turtles play together, and they love swimming in their aquarium.

5. My bird's name is Sweetie. She likes sitting on my hand.
   My bird's name is Sweetie, and she likes sitting on my hand.

Write a compound sentence. Remember to write a coordinating conjunction in the sentence, and write a comma before the conjunction.

6. Answers will vary.

Pets

Page 48

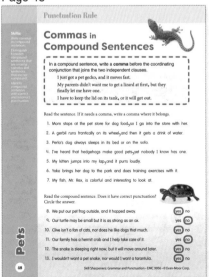

Commas in Compound Sentences

In a compound sentence, write a **comma** before the coordinating conjunction that joins the two independent clauses.

I just got a pet gecko, and it moves fast.
My parents didn't want me to get a lizard at first, but they finally let me have one.
I have to keep the lid on its tank, or it will get out.

Read the sentence. If it needs a comma, write a comma where it belongs.

1. Mom stops at the pet store for dog food, so I go into the store with her.
2. A gerbil runs frantically on its wheel, and then it gets a drink of water.
3. Perla's dog always sleeps in its bed or on the sofa.
4. I've heard that hedgehogs make good pets, yet nobody I know has one.
5. My kitten jumps into my lap, and it purrs loudly.
6. Yoko brings her dog to the park and does training exercises with it.
7. My fish, Mr. Rex, is colorful and interesting to look at.

Read the compound sentence. Does it have correct punctuation? Circle the answer.

8. We put our pet frog outside, and it hopped away.   **yes**   no
9. Our turtle may be small but it is as strong as an ox.   yes   **no**
10. Clive isn't a fan of cats, nor does he like dogs that much.   **yes**   no
11. Our family has a hermit crab and I help take care of it.   yes   **no**
12. The snake is sleeping right now, but it will move around later.   **yes**   no
13. I wouldn't want a pet snake, nor would I want a tarantula.   **yes**   no

Pets

Page 49

What's Happening?

There are 15 fish in the aquarium. Use the words inside the fish to make 6 compound sentences. Write each sentence on a line, and remember to write a comma where it is needed.

1. Answers will vary.
2. Answers will vary.
3. Answers will vary.
4. Answers will vary.
5. Answers will vary.
6. Answers will vary.

Pets

Page 50

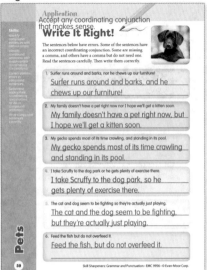

Application
Accept any coordinating conjunction that makes sense.

Write It Right!

The sentences below have errors. Some of the sentences have an incorrect coordinating conjunction. Some are missing a comma, and others have a comma but do not need one. Read the sentences carefully. Then write them correctly.

1. Surfer runs around and barks, nor he chews up our furniture!
   Surfer runs around and barks, and he chews up our furniture!

2. My family doesn't have a pet right now nor I hope we'll get a kitten soon.
   My family doesn't have a pet right now, but I hope we'll get a kitten soon.

3. My gecko spends most of its time crawling, and standing in its pool.
   My gecko spends most of its time crawling and standing in its pool.

4. I take Scruffy to the dog park or he gets plenty of exercise there.
   I take Scruffy to the dog park, so he gets plenty of exercise there.

5. The cat and dog seem to be fighting so they're actually just playing.
   The cat and the dog seem to be fighting, but they're actually just playing.

6. Feed the fish but do not overfeed it.
   Feed the fish, but do not overfeed it.

Page 51

What Pet Should I Get?

Read the sentences, and write commas in the compound sentences where they belong.

1. I'm getting a new pet, but I haven't decided what kind I want.
2. I have two different animals in mind and will have to choose one.
3. I promised my parents I'd feed my pet and take good care of it.
4. They said we can go to the pet store on Saturday and pick out a pet.
5. I would be happy with either pet, and I know that both pets will need attention.
6. This will be my first pet, so I can hardly wait for the weekend to arrive.
7. We'll need some supplies and other things for my new pet.
8. We can buy the supplies at the pet store, or we can order them online.
9. I've been reading about both animals and understand what they will need.
10. I spend time after school and after dinner reading or watching videos online.
11. My friend Chang will come over, and we'll play with my pet.
12. Chang loves animals and has a pet snake of his own.
13. I know I have to wait until Saturday, but it's going to be hard to wait that long!

On the lines below, write the green letters from the sentences you added commas to.

b i t l b a i r e g r b

What are the two animals that I may get as a pet? Unscramble the letters you wrote above. Write them to complete the sentence below.

I will get a ___rabbit___ or a ___gerbil___.

Page 52

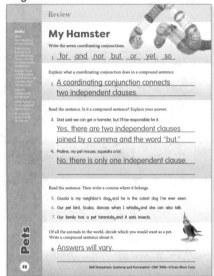

Review

My Hamster

Write the seven coordinating conjunctions.

1. _for_ _and_ _nor_ _but_ _or_ _yet_ _so_

Explain what a coordinating conjunction does in a compound sentence.

2. A coordinating conjunction connects two independent clauses.

Read the sentence. Is it a compound sentence? Explain your answer.

3. Dad said we can get a hamster, but I'll be responsible for it.
   Yes, there are two independent clauses joined by a comma and the word "but."

4. Praline, my pet mouse, squeaks a lot.
   No, there is only one independent clause.

Read the sentence. Then write a comma where it belongs.

5. Gouda is my neighbor's dog, and he is the cutest dog I've ever seen.
6. Our pet bird, Scuba, dances when I whistle, and she can also talk.
7. Our family has a pet tarantula, and it eats insects.

Of all the animals in the world, decide which you would want as a pet. Write a compound sentence about it.

8. Answers will vary.

Page 53

Story

Read the story.

Tough Competition

When the buzzer sounds, I take off. Another racer takes the lead. With my racing mitts on my hands, I furiously spin my chair's wheels and try to close the gap between me and her. I fly across the pavement as the crowd cheers.

I use a wheelchair because I have a joint condition. Before I got into racing, I spent a lot of time searching for a sport that I'd enjoy playing in my wheelchair. I am very competitive! Whenever I'm racing, I feel limitless and tough. I know I can do anything. When I race, I focus on just one thing: winning. As we approach the halfway point, my arms begin to tire. Until I reach the finish line, there's no slowing down! That girl is still in the lead. Unless I pick up the pace, she'll win. I go faster and faster, but it isn't enough. I come in just after her. After the race is over, she smiles and says I'm tough competition. I smile and tell her I'll be even tougher next time!

Read the rules. Answer the questions.

Grammar A subordinating conjunction begins a dependent clause that joins an independent clause to form a complex sentence.

How many purple subordinating conjunctions and green complex sentences can you find in the story?
__9__ subordinating conjunctions   __9__ complex sentences

Punctuation We write a comma (,) after the dependent clause when it is at the beginning of a complex sentence.

How many orange commas can you find in the story? __7__

Page 54

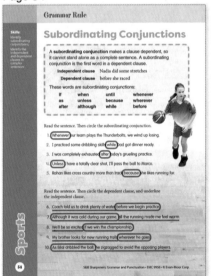

Grammar Rule

Subordinating Conjunctions

A subordinating conjunction makes a clause dependent, so it cannot stand alone as a complete thought. A subordinating conjunction is the first word in a dependent clause.

Independent clause Nadia did some stretches
Dependent clause before she raced

These words are subordinating conjunctions:

if	when	until	whenever
as	unless	because	wherever
after	although	while	before

Read the sentence. Then circle the subordinating conjunction.

1. (Whenever) our team plays the Thunderbolts, we wind up losing.
2. I practiced some dribbling skills (while) Dad got dinner ready.
3. I was completely exhausted (after) today's grueling practice.
4. (Unless) I have a totally clear shot, I'll pass the ball to Marco.
5. Rohan likes cross country more than track (because) he likes running far.

Read the sentence. Then circle the dependent clause, and underline the independent clause.

6. Coach told us to drink plenty of water (before we begin practice).
7. (Although it was cold during our game,) all the running made me feel warm.
8. We'll be so excited (if we win the championship).
9. My brother looks for new running trails (wherever he goes).
10. As Bilal dribbled the ball, he zigzagged to avoid the opposing players.

Page 55

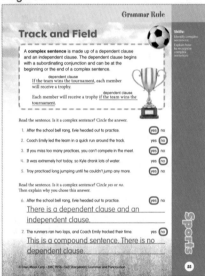

Grammar Rule

Track and Field

A complex sentence is made up of a dependent clause and an independent clause. The dependent clause begins with a subordinating conjunction and can be at the beginning or the end of a complex sentence.

dependent clause
If the team wins the tournament, each member will receive a trophy.

dependent clause
Each member will receive a trophy if the team wins the tournament.

Read the sentence. Is it a complex sentence? Circle the answer.

1. After the school bell rang, Evie headed out to practice. (yes) no
2. Coach Emily led the team in a quick run around the track. yes (no)
3. If you miss too many practices, you can't compete in the meet. (yes) no
4. It was extremely hot today, so Kyle drank lots of water. yes (no)
5. Troy practiced long jumping until he couldn't jump any more. (yes) no

Read the sentence. Is it a complex sentence? Circle yes or no. Then explain why you chose that answer.

6. After the school bell rang, Evie headed out to practice. (yes) no
   There is a dependent clause and an independent clause.

7. The runners ran two laps, and Coach Emily tracked their time. yes (no)
   This is a compound sentence. There is no dependent clause.

Page 56

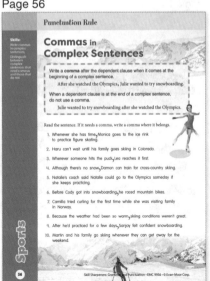

Punctuation Rule

Commas in Complex Sentences

Write a **comma** after the dependent clause when it comes at the beginning of a complex sentence.

After she watched the Olympics, Julie wanted to try snowboarding.

When a dependent clause is at the end of a complex sentence, do not use a comma.

Julie wanted to try snowboarding after she watched the Olympics.

Read the sentence. If it needs a comma, write a comma where it belongs.

1. Whenever she has time, Monica goes to the ice rink to practice figure skating.
2. Haru can't wait until his family goes skiing in Colorado.
3. Wherever someone hits the puck, Lea reaches it first.
4. Although there's no snow, Damon can train for cross-country skiing.
5. Natalie's coach said Natalie could go to the Olympics someday if she keeps practicing.
6. Before Cody got into snowboarding, he raced mountain bikes.
7. Camilla tried curling for the first time while she was visiting family in Norway.
8. Because the weather had been so warm, skiing conditions weren't great.
9. After he'd practiced for a few days, Sanjay felt confident snowboarding.
10. Martin and his family go skiing whenever they can get away for the weekend.

Page 57

Grammar Fun

Soccer Practice

Today's soccer practice is tough! Read the sentences. Some sentences are complex, and others are not. To get the ball down the field, draw a line through all the complex sentences. Avoid any sentences that are not complex.

Page 58

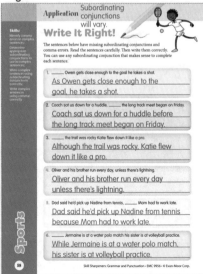

Application
Subordinating conjunctions will vary.

Write It Right!

The sentences below have missing subordinating conjunctions and comma errors. Read the sentences carefully. Then write them correctly. You can use any subordinating conjunction that makes sense to complete each sentence.

1. ___ Owen gets close enough to the goal he takes a shot.
   As Owen gets close enough to the goal, he takes a shot.

2. Coach sat us down for a huddle, ___ the long track meet began on Friday.
   Coach sat us down for a huddle before the long track meet began on Friday.

3. ___ the trail was rocky Katie flew down it like a pro.
   Although the trail was rocky, Katie flew down it like a pro.

4. Oliver and his brother run every day, unless there's lightning.
   Oliver and his brother run every day unless there's lightning.

5. Dad said he'd pick up Nadine from tennis, ___ Mom had to work late.
   Dad said he'd pick up Nadine from tennis because Mom had to work late.

6. ___ Jermaine is at a water polo match his sister is at volleyball practice.
   While Jermaine is at a water polo match, his sister is at volleyball practice.

Page 59

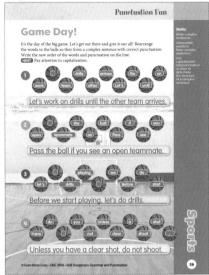

Punctuation Fun

Game Day!

It's the day of the big game. Let's get out there and give it our all! Rearrange the words in the balls so they form a complex sentence with correct punctuation. Write the new order of the words and punctuation on the line.

HINT Pay attention to capitalization.

1. Let's work on drills until the other team arrives.

2. Pass the ball if you see an open teammate.

3. Before we start playing, let's do drills.

4. Unless you have a clear shot, do not shoot.

Page 60

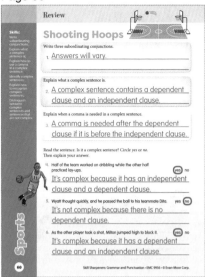

Review

Shooting Hoops

Write three subordinating conjunctions.

1. Answers will vary.

Explain what a complex sentence is.

2. A complex sentence contains a dependent clause and an independent clause.

Explain when a comma is needed in a complex sentence.

3. A comma is needed after the dependent clause if it is before the independent clause.

Read the sentence. Is it a complex sentence? Circle yes or no. Then explain your answer.

4. Half of the team worked on dribbling while the other half practiced lay-ups. **(yes)** no
   It's complex because it has an independent clause and a dependent clause.

5. Wyatt thought quickly, and he passed the ball to his teammate Dita. yes **(no)**
   It's not complex because there is no dependent clause.

6. As the other player took a shot, Milton jumped high to block it. **(yes)** no
   It's complex because it has a dependent clause and an independent clause.

Page 61

Story

Read the story.

Beach Day!

Saturday morning, I awoke early. I washed my face, brushed my teeth, and found my bathing suit. Then I went outside to help Dad. He was loading coolers, blankets, towels, and other gear into our car. My little sister, Eliza, was running around, loudly singing every "beach" word she knows. "Sand, waves, and seashells!" She really loves the beach. We go frequently in the summer, but this was the first time this season, and I don't think Dad had planned well. Mom came over and carefully examined everything. It turns out Dad hadn't packed snacks, water bottles, or extra clothes. We quickly gathered those items. Eliza, meanwhile, was still singing: "Flip-flops, clouds, and sharks!"

"That is definitely everything," he said confidently. We were now in the car and ready to go! Halfway down the driveway, Eliza sang, "Seabirds, sea stars, and sunscreen!" Dad stopped the car and laughed. "Thanks, Eliza! I totally forgot the sunscreen!"

Read the rules. Answer the questions.

Grammar An adverb describes how, when, or where an action happens. Adverbs can also describe adjectives, phrases, and clauses.

How many blue adverbs can you find in the story? 14

Punctuation Write a comma (,) to separate each item in a series. A series is a list of three or more items. Each item can be a single word or a phrase.

How many orange commas can you find in the story? 13

Page 62

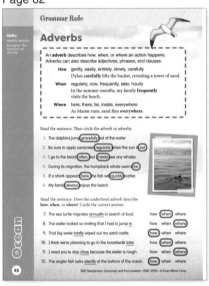

Grammar Rule

Adverbs

An **adverb** describes how, when, or where an action happens. Adverbs can also describe adjectives, phrases, and clauses.

How gently, easily, entirely, slowly, carefully
Dylan **carefully** lifts the bucket, revealing a tower of sand.

When regularly, now, frequently, later, hourly
In the summer months, my family **frequently** visits the beach.

Where here, there, far, inside, everywhere
As Maisie runs, sand flies **everywhere**.

Read the sentence. Then circle the adverb or adverbs.

1. The dolphins jump (gracefully) out of the water.
2. Be sure to apply sunscreen (regularly) when the sun is out.
3. I go to the beach (often), but I (rarely) see any whales.
4. During its migration, the humpback whale swims (far).
5. If a shark appears (here), the fish will (quickly) scatter.
6. My family (always) enjoys the beach.

Read the sentence. Does the underlined adverb describe how, when, or where? Circle the correct answer.

7. The sea turtle migrates annually in search of food. how **(when)** where
8. The water looked so inviting that I had to jump in. how when **(where)**
9. That big wave totally wiped out my sand castle. **(how)** when where
10. I think we're planning to go to the boardwalk later. how **(when)** where
11. I need you to stay close because the water is rough. how when **(where)**
12. The angler fish lurks silently at the bottom of the ocean. **(how)** when where

Page 63

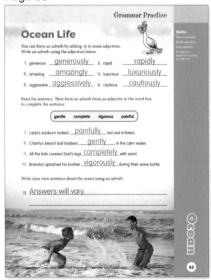

Grammar Practice

Ocean Life

You can form an adverb by adding -ly to some adjectives. Write an adverb using the adjectives below.

1. generous — generously
2. rapid — rapidly
3. amazing — amazingly
4. luxurious — luxuriously
5. aggressive — aggressively
6. cautious — cautiously

Read the sentence. Then form an adverb from an adjective in the word box to complete the sentence.

[gentle   complete   vigorous   painful]

7. Layla's sunburn looked painfully red and irritated.
8. Charity's beach ball bobbed gently in the calm water.
9. All the kids covered Dad's legs completely with sand.
10. Brandon splashed his brother vigorously during their wave battle.

Write your own sentence about the ocean using an adverb.

11. Answers will vary.

Page 64

Punctuation Rule

Commas with Items in a Series

Use **commas** to separate each item in a series, or list, of three or more items. An item can be a noun, a verb, an adjective, or another part of speech. A comma always goes before and or in a series.

We saw crabs, pelicans, seagulls, and dolphins while at the beach today.

An item can be a single word or a phrase.

Series with words blanket, umbrella, and cooler
Series with phrases walk in the sand, splash in the waves, or lie in the sun

Read the series. Then write commas to separate the items in the series.

1. sunscreen, sunglasses, and flip-flops
2. swim, splash, or dive
3. take a walk, go for a swim, or nap on the blanket
4. float on a raft, go out on a boat, and surf the waves
5. arrived early, spent the day on the beach, and went to the boardwalk at night

Read the sentence. Then write commas to separate the items in the series.

6. Fish, sea sponges, and sea slugs can all be found in a coral reef.
7. A crab pinched me, a wave knocked me over, and a beach ball hit me.
8. The beach was dazzling, peaceful, and exhilarating.
9. I spent the day at the beach with my friends Diego, Rupert, Darcy, and Chang.
10. We went snorkeling, surfing, and swimming today.

Page 65

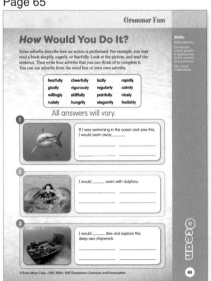

Grammar Fun

How Would You Do It?

Some adverbs describe how an action is performed. For example, you may read a book sleepily, eagerly, or fearfully. Look at the picture, and read the sentence. Then write four adverbs that you can think of to complete it. You can use adverbs from the word box or your own adverbs.

[fearfully   cheerfully   lazily   rapidly
gladly   vigorously   regularly   calmly
willingly   skillfully   painfully   nicely
rudely   hungrily   elegantly   foolishly]

All answers will vary.

1. If I was swimming in the ocean and saw this, I would swim away _____

2. I would _____ swim with dolphins.

3. I would _____ dive and explore this deep-sea shipwreck.

Page 66

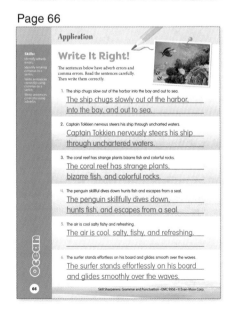

Application

Write It Right!

The sentences below have adverb errors and comma errors. Read the sentences carefully. Then write them correctly.

1. The ship chugs slow out of the harbor into the bay and out to sea.
   The ship chugs slowly out of the harbor, into the bay, and out to sea.

2. Captain Tokkien nervous steers his ship through uncharted waters.
   Captain Tokkien nervously steers his ship through unchartered waters.

3. The coral reef has strange plants bizarre fish and colorful rocks.
   The coral reef has strange plants, bizarre fish, and colorful rocks.

4. The penguin skillful dives down hunts fish and escapes from a seal.
   The penguin skillfully dives down, hunts fish, and escapes from a seal.

5. The air is cool salty fishy and refreshing.
   The air is cool, salty, fishy, and refreshing.

6. The surfer stands effortless on his board and glides smooth over the waves.
   The surfer stands effortlessly on his board and glides smoothly over the waves.

Page 67

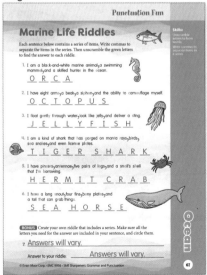

Punctuation Fun

Marine Life Riddles

Each sentence below contains a series of items. Write commas to separate the items in the series. Then unscramble the green letters to find the answer to each riddle.

1. I am a black-and-white marine animal, a swimming mammal, and a skilled hunter in the ocean.
   O R C A

2. I have eight arms, a beak, a siphon, and the ability to camouflage myself.
   O C T O P U S

3. I float gently through water, look like jelly, and deliver a sting.
   J E L L Y F I S H

4. I am a kind of shark that has gorged on manta rays, birds, sea snakes, and even license plates.
   T I G E R S H A R K

5. I have pincers, antennae, five pairs of legs, and a snail's shell that I'm borrowing.
   H E R M I T C R A B

6. I have a long snout, four fins, bony plates, and a tail that can grab things.
   S E A H O R S E

BONUS Create your own riddle that includes a series. Make sure all the letters you need for the answer are included in your sentence, and circle the answer.

7. Answers will vary.

Answer to your riddle: Answers will vary.

Page 68

Page 69

Page 70

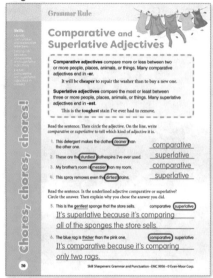

Page 71

Page 72

Page 73

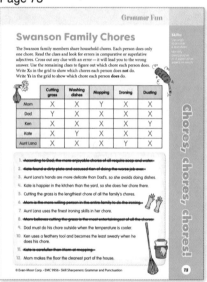

Page 74

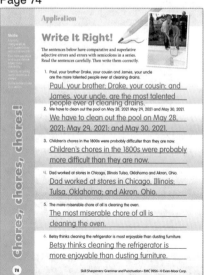

Page 75

Page 76

To download a larger version of this answer key, go to: ***www.evan-moor.com/resources***
Enter your email address and this resource code: **EMC9956**

Page 77

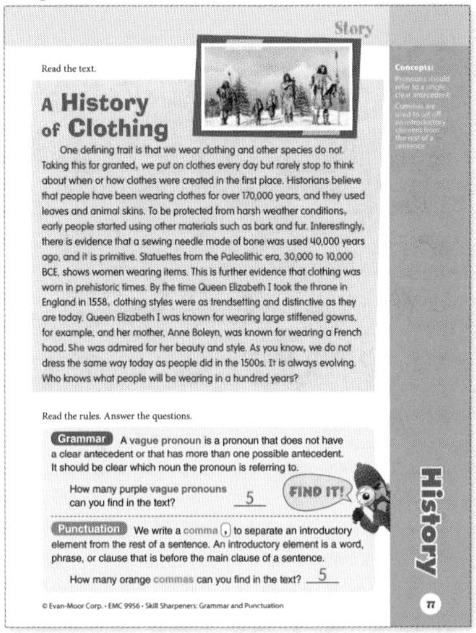

Story

Read the text.

A History of Clothing

One defining trait is that we wear clothing and other species do not. Taking this for granted, we put on clothes every day but rarely stop to think about when or how clothes were created in the first place. Historians believe that people have been wearing clothes for over 170,000 years, and they used leaves and animal skins. To be protected from harsh weather conditions, early people started using other materials such as bark and fur. Interestingly, there is evidence that a sewing needle made of bone was used 40,000 years ago, and it is primitive. Statuettes from the Paleolithic era, 30,000 to 10,000 BCE, shows women wearing items. This is further evidence that clothing was worn in prehistoric times. By the time Queen Elizabeth I took the throne in England in 1558, clothing styles were as trendsetting and distinctive as they are today. Queen Elizabeth I was known for wearing large stiffened gowns, for example, and her mother, Anne Boleyn, was known for wearing a French hood. She was admired for her beauty and style. As you know, we do not dress the same way today as people did in the 1500s. It is always evolving. Who knows what people will be wearing in a hundred years?

Read the rules. Answer the questions.

Grammar A vague pronoun is a pronoun that does not have a clear antecedent or that has more than one possible antecedent. It should be clear which noun the pronoun is referring to.

How many purple vague pronouns can you find in the text? 5

Punctuation We write a comma (,) to separate an introductory element from the rest of a sentence. An introductory element is a word, phrase, or clause that is before the main clause of the sentence.

How many orange commas can you find in the text? 5

History

© Evan-Moor Corp. • EMC 9956 • Skill Sharpeners: Grammar and Punctuation 77

Page 78

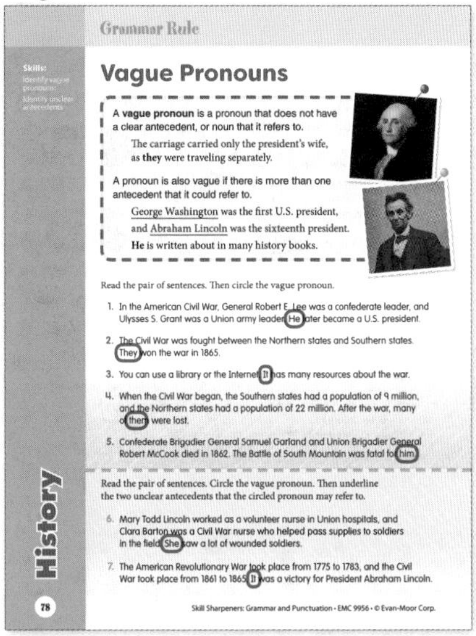

Grammar Rule

Vague Pronouns

A **vague pronoun** is a pronoun that does not have a clear antecedent, or noun that it refers to.
The carriage carried only the president's wife, as **they** were traveling separately.

A pronoun is also vague if there is more than one antecedent that it could refer to.
George Washington was the first U.S. president, and Abraham Lincoln was the sixteenth president. **He** is written about in many history books.

Read the pair of sentences. Then circle the vague pronoun.

1. In the American Civil War, General Robert E. Lee was a confederate leader, and Ulysses S. Grant was a Union army leader. (He) later became a U.S. president.
2. The Civil War was fought between the Northern states and Southern states. (They) won the war in 1865.
3. You can use a library or the Internet. (It) has many resources about the war.
4. When the Civil War began, the Southern states had a population of 9 million, and the Northern states had a population of 22 million. After the war, many of (them) were lost.
5. Confederate Brigadier General Samuel Garland and Union Brigadier General Robert McCook died in 1862. The Battle of South Mountain was fatal for (him).

Read the pair of sentences. Circle the vague pronoun. Then underline the two unclear antecedents that the circled pronoun may refer to.

6. Mary Todd Lincoln worked as a volunteer nurse in Union hospitals, and Clara Barton was a Civil War nurse who helped pass supplies to soldiers in the field. (She) saw a lot of wounded soldiers.
7. The American Revolutionary War took place from 1775 to 1783, and the Civil War took place from 1861 to 1865. (It) was a victory for President Abraham Lincoln.

History

78 Skill Sharpeners: Grammar and Punctuation • EMC 9956 • © Evan-Moor Corp.

Page 79

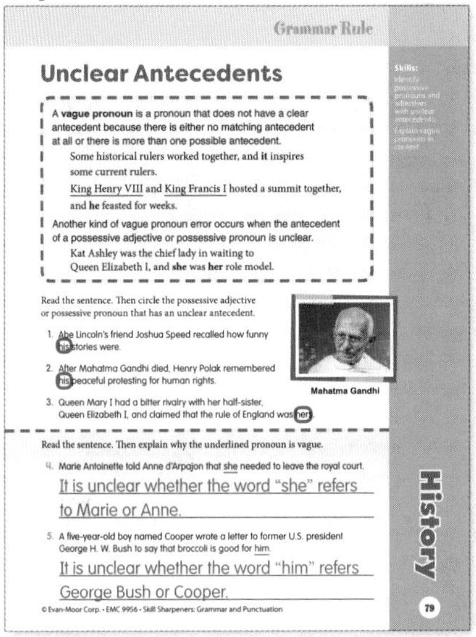

Grammar Rule

Unclear Antecedents

A **vague pronoun** is a pronoun that does not have a clear antecedent because there is either no matching antecedent at all or there is more than one possible antecedent.
Some historical rulers worked together, and **it** inspires some current rulers.
King Henry VIII and King Francis I hosted a summit together, and **he** feasted for weeks.

Another kind of vague pronoun error occurs when the antecedent of a possessive adjective or possessive pronoun is unclear.
Kat Ashley was the chief lady in waiting to Queen Elizabeth I, and **she** was **her** role model.

Read the sentence. Then circle the possessive adjective or possessive pronoun that has an unclear antecedent.

1. Abe Lincoln's friend Joshua Speed recalled how funny (his) stories were.
2. After Mahatma Gandhi died, Henry Polak remembered (his) peaceful protesting for human rights.
3. Queen Mary I had a bitter rivalry with her half-sister, Queen Elizabeth I, and claimed that the rule of England was (hers).

Mahatma Gandhi

Read the sentence. Then explain why the underlined pronoun is vague.

4. Marie Antoinette told Anne d'Arpajon that she needed to leave the royal court.
It is unclear whether the word "she" refers to Marie or Anne.
5. A five-year-old boy named Cooper wrote a letter to former U.S. president George H. W. Bush to say that broccoli is good for him.
It is unclear whether the word "him" refers George Bush or Cooper.

History

© Evan-Moor Corp. • EMC 9956 • Skill Sharpeners: Grammar and Punctuation 79

Page 80

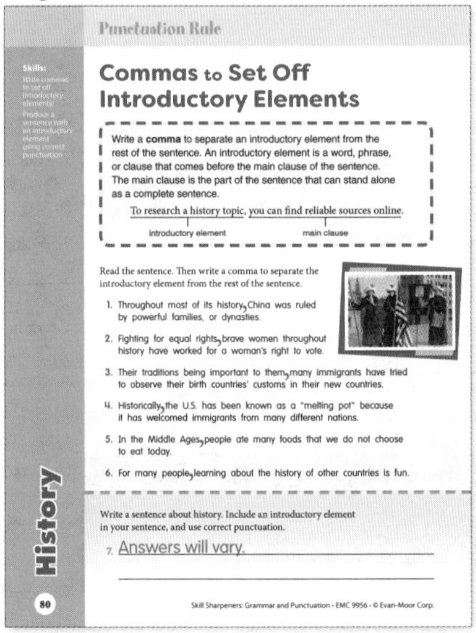

Punctuation Rule

Commas to Set Off Introductory Elements

Write a **comma** to separate an introductory element from the rest of the sentence. An introductory element is a word, phrase, or clause that comes before the main clause of the sentence. The main clause is the part of the sentence that can stand alone as a complete sentence.
To research a history topic, you can find reliable sources online.
(introductory element / main clause)

Read the sentence. Then write a comma to separate the introductory element from the rest of the sentence.

1. Throughout most of its history, China was ruled by powerful families, or dynasties.
2. Fighting for equal rights, brave women throughout history have worked for a woman's right to vote.
3. Their traditions being important to them, many immigrants have tried to observe their birth countries' customs in their new countries.
4. Historically, the U.S. has been known as a "melting pot" because it has welcomed immigrants from many different nations.
5. In the Middle Ages, people ate many foods that we do not choose to eat today.
6. For many people, learning about the history of other countries is fun.

Write a sentence about history. Include an introductory element in your sentence, and use correct punctuation.

7. Answers will vary.

History

80 Skill Sharpeners: Grammar and Punctuation • EMC 9956 • © Evan-Moor Corp.

Page 81

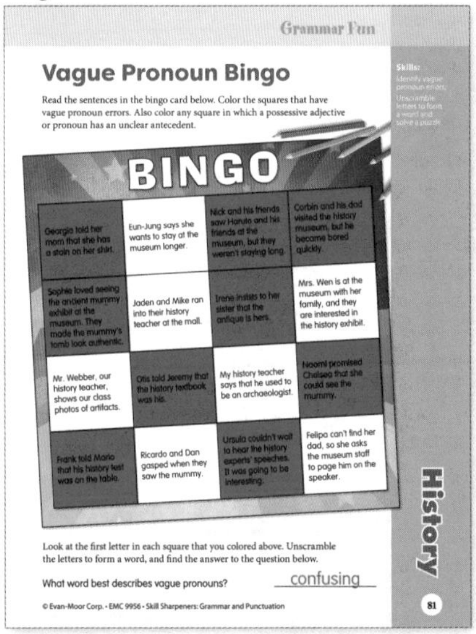

Grammar Fun

Vague Pronoun Bingo

Read the sentences in the bingo card below. Color the squares that have vague pronoun errors. Also color any square in which a possessive adjective or pronoun has an unclear antecedent.

BINGO

Georgia told her mom that she has a stain on her shirt.	Eun-Jung says she wants to stay at the museum longer.	Nick and his friends saw Haruto and his friends at the museum, but they weren't staying long.	Corbin and his dad visited the history museum, but he becomes bored quickly.
Sophie loved seeing the ancient mummy exhibit at the museum. They made the mummy's tomb look authentic.	Jaden and Mike ran into their history teacher at the mall.	Irene insists to her sister that the antique is hers.	Mrs. Wen is at the museum with her family, and they are interested in the history exhibit.
Mr. Webber, our history teacher, shows our class photos of artifacts.	Otis told Jeremy that the history textbook was his.	My history teacher says that he used to be an archaeologist.	Naomi promised Chelsea that she could see the mummy.
Frank told Mario that his history test was on the table.	Ricardo and Dan gasped when they saw the mummy.	Ursula couldn't wait to hear the history experts' speeches. It was going to be interesting.	Felipe can't find her dad, so she asks the museum staff to page him on the speaker.

Look at the first letter in each square that you colored above. Unscramble the letters to form a word, and find the answer to the question below.

What word best describes vague pronouns? confusing

History

© Evan-Moor Corp. • EMC 9956 • Skill Sharpeners: Grammar and Punctuation 81

Page 82

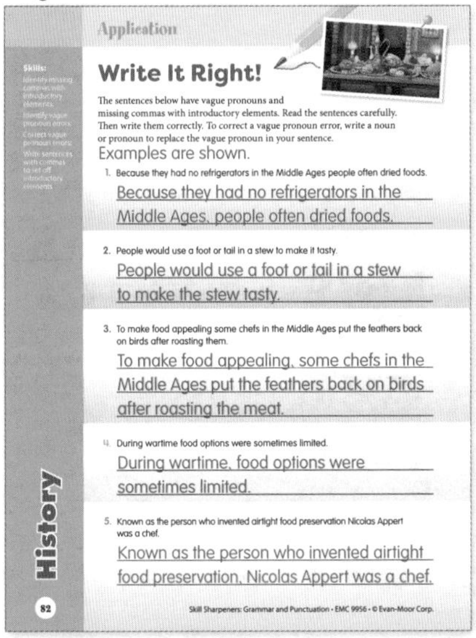

Application

Write It Right!

The sentences below have vague pronouns and missing commas with introductory elements. Read the sentences carefully. Then write them correctly. To correct a vague pronoun error, write a noun or pronoun to replace the vague pronoun in your sentence.

Examples are shown.

1. Because they had no refrigerators in the Middle Ages people often dried foods.
Because they had no refrigerators in the Middle Ages, people often dried foods.
2. People would use a foot or tail in a stew to make it tasty.
People would use a foot or tail in a stew to make the stew tasty.
3. To make food appealing some chefs in the Middle Ages put the feathers back on birds after roasting them.
To make food appealing, some chefs in the Middle Ages put the feathers back on birds after roasting the meat.
4. During wartime food options were sometimes limited.
During wartime, food options were sometimes limited.
5. Known as the person who invented airtight food preservation Nicolas Appert was a chef.
Known as the person who invented airtight food preservation, Nicolas Appert was a chef.

History

82 Skill Sharpeners: Grammar and Punctuation • EMC 9956 • © Evan-Moor Corp.

Page 83

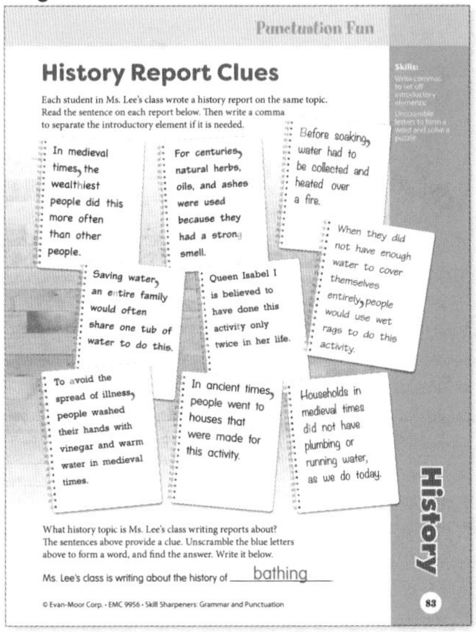

Punctuation Fun

History Report Clues

Each student in Ms. Lee's class wrote a history report on the same topic. Read the sentence on each report below. Then write a comma to separate the introductory element if it is needed.

- In medieval times, the wealthiest people did this more often than other people.
- For centuries, natural herbs, oils, and ashes were used because they had a strong smell.
- Before soaking, water had to be collected and heated over a fire.
- When they did not have enough water to cover themselves entirely, people would use wet rags to do this activity.
- Saving water, an entire family would often share one tub of water to do this.
- Queen Isabel I is believed to have done this activity only twice in her life.
- To avoid the spread of illness, people washed their hands with vinegar and warm water in medieval times.
- In ancient times, people went to houses that were made for this activity.
- Households in medieval times did not have plumbing or running water, as we do today.

What history topic is Ms. Lee's class writing reports about? The sentences above provide a clue. Unscramble the blue letters to form a word, and find the answer. Write it below.

Ms. Lee's class is writing about the history of bathing

History

© Evan-Moor Corp. • EMC 9956 • Skill Sharpeners: Grammar and Punctuation 83

Page 84

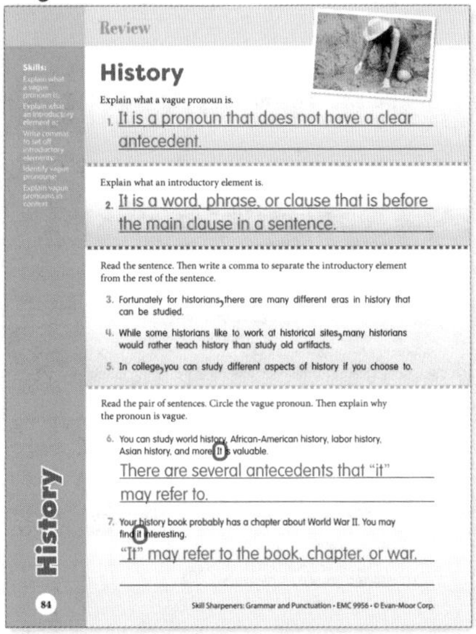

Review

History

Explain what a vague pronoun is.

1. It is a pronoun that does not have a clear antecedent.

Explain what an introductory element is.

2. It is a word, phrase, or clause that is before the main clause in a sentence.

Read the sentence. Then write a comma to separate the introductory element from the rest of the sentence.

3. Fortunately for historians, there are many different eras in history that can be studied.
4. While some historians like to work at historical sites, many historians would rather teach history than study old artifacts.
5. In college, you can study different aspects of history if you choose to.

Read the pair of sentences. Circle the vague pronoun. Then explain why the pronoun is vague.

6. You can study world history, African-American history, labor history, Asian history, and more. (It) is valuable.
There are several antecedents that "it" may refer to.
7. Your history book probably has a chapter about World War II. You may find (it) interesting.
"It" may refer to the book, chapter, or war.

History

84 Skill Sharpeners: Grammar and Punctuation • EMC 9956 • © Evan-Moor Corp.

Page 85

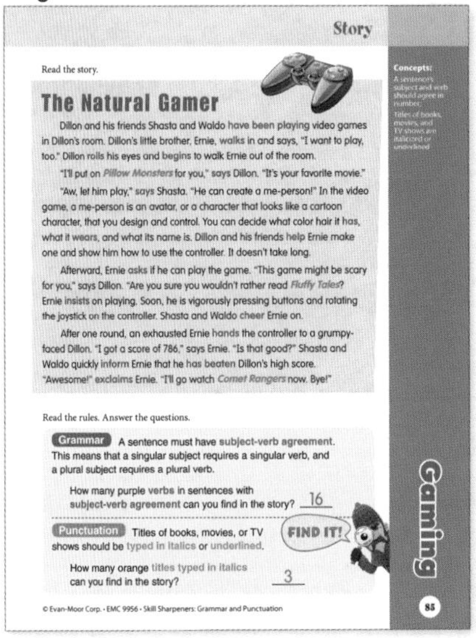

Story

Read the story.

The Natural Gamer

Dillon and his friends Shasta and Waldo have been playing video games in Dillon's room. Dillon's little brother, Ernie, walks in and says, "I want to play, too." Dillon rolls his eyes and begins to walk Ernie out of the room.

"I'll put on *Pillow Monsters* for you," says Dillon. "It's your favorite movie."

"Aw, let him play," says Shasta. "He can create a me-person!" In the video game, a me-person is an avatar, or a character that looks like a cartoon character, that you design and control. You can decide what color hair it has, what it wears, and what its name is. Dillon and his friends help Ernie make one and show him how to use the controller. It doesn't take long.

Afterward, Ernie asks if he can play the game. "This game might be scary for you," says Dillon. "Are you sure you wouldn't rather read *Fluffy Tales*?" Ernie insists on playing. Soon, he is vigorously pressing buttons and rotating the joystick on the controller. Shasta and Waldo cheer Ernie on.

After one round, an exhausted Ernie hands the controller to a grumpy-faced Dillon. "I got a score of 786," says Ernie. "Is that good?" Shasta and Waldo quickly inform Ernie that he has beaten Dillon's high score.

"Awesome!" exclaims Ernie. "I'll go watch *Comet Rangers* now. Bye!"

Read the rules. Answer the questions.

Grammar A sentence must have subject-verb agreement. This means that a singular subject requires a singular verb, and a plural subject requires a plural verb.

How many purple verbs in sentences with subject-verb agreement can you find in the story? 16

Punctuation Titles of books, movies, or TV shows should be typed in italics or underlined.

How many orange titles typed in italics can you find in the story? 3

Gaming

© Evan-Moor Corp. • EMC 9956 • Skill Sharpeners: Grammar and Punctuation 85

Page 86

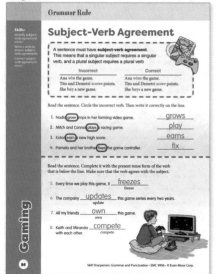

Grammar Rule

Subject-Verb Agreement

A sentence must have **subject-verb agreement.** This means that a singular subject requires a singular verb, and a plural subject requires a plural verb.

Incorrect	Correct
Ana win the game.	Ana wins the game.
Tito and Demetri scores points.	Tito and Demetri score points.
She buy a new game.	She buys a new game.

Read the sentence. Circle the incorrect verb. Then write it correctly on the line.

1. Nadia ~~grows~~ crops in her farming video game. — **grows**
2. Mitch and Connor ~~plays~~ a racing game. — **play**
3. Kotori ~~earn~~ a new high score. — **earns**
4. Pamela and her brother ~~fixes~~ the game controller. — **fix**

Read the sentence. Complete it with the present tense form of the verb that is below the line. Make sure that the verb agrees with the subject.

5. Every time we play this game, it **freezes** (freeze)
6. The company **updates** this game series every two years. (update)
7. All my friends **own** this game. (own)
8. Keith and Miranda **compete** with each other. (compete)

Page 87

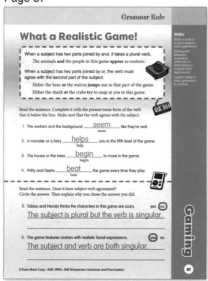

Grammar Rule

What a Realistic Game!

When a subject has two parts joined by *and*, it takes a plural verb. The animals **and** the people in this game **appear** so realistic.

When a subject has two parts joined by *or*, the verb must agree with the second part of the subject.
Either the bear or the walrus **jumps** out in that part of the game.
Either the shark **or** the crabs **try** to snap at you in this game.

Read the sentence. Complete it with the present tense form of the verb that is below the line. Make sure that the verb agrees with the subject.

1. The avatars and the background **seem** like they're real. (seem)
2. A monster or a fairy **helps** you in the fifth level of the game. (help)
3. The house or the trees **begin** to move in the game. (begin)
4. Pritty and Deeta **beat** the game every time they play. (beat)

Read the sentence. Does it have subject-verb agreement? Circle the answer. Then explain why you chose the answer you did.

5. Tobias and Honda thinks the characters in this game are scary. **no**
   The subject is plural but the verb is singular.

6. The game features avatars with realistic facial expressions. **yes**
   The subject and verb are both singular.

Page 88

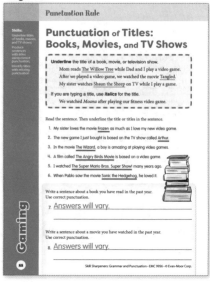

Punctuation Rule

Punctuation of Titles: Books, Movies, and TV Shows

Underline the title of a book, movie, or television show.
Mom reads <u>The Willow Tree</u> while Dad and I play a video game.
After we played a video game, we watched the movie <u>Shaun the Sheep</u> on TV while I play a game.

If you are typing a title, use *italics* for the title.
We watched *Moana* after playing our fitness video game.

Read the sentence. Then underline the title or titles in the sentence.

1. My sister loves the movie <u>Frozen</u> as much as I love my new video game.
2. The new game I just bought is based on the TV show called <u>Arthur</u>.
3. In the movie <u>The Wizard</u>, a boy is amazing at playing video games.
4. A film called <u>The Angry Birds Movie</u> is based on a video game.
5. I watched <u>The Super Mario Bros. Super Show!</u> many years ago.
6. When Pablo saw the movie <u>Sonic the Hedgehog</u>, he loved it.

Write a sentence about a book you have read in the past year. Use correct punctuation.

7. Answers will vary.

Write a sentence about a movie you have watched in the past year. Use correct punctuation.

8. Answers will vary.

Page 89

Grammar Fun

So Many Avatars!

Look at the video game picture. Then write a verb phrase to complete each sentence, and tell what is happening in the picture. Use a different verb in each sentence, and make sure each sentence has subject-verb agreement.

1. The boy and the dinosaur — Answers will vary.
2. A monster — Answers will vary.
3. The people playing this game — Answers will vary.
4. The car — Answers will vary.

Page 90

Application

Write It Right!

The sentences below have subject-verb agreement errors and title punctuation errors. Read the sentences carefully. Then write them correctly.

1. Mojgan and Roya plays a game based on the book Rapid Flotation Race.
   Mojgan and Roya play a game based on the book Rapid Flotation Race.

2. Jakwon or Kim win this game every time.
   Jakwon or Kim wins this game every time.

3. Ceaser loves the movie The Golden Compass, and he also likes the game.
   Ceaser loves the movie The Golden Compass, and he also likes the game.

4. This game have puzzles and clues and are based on the TV show Spy Kids.
   This game has puzzles and clues and is based on the TV show Spy Kids.

5. All these games is familiar because I've played them before.
   All these games are familiar because I've played them before.

6. My brother attempt to play a new video game every week.
   My brother attempts to play a new video game every week.

Page 91

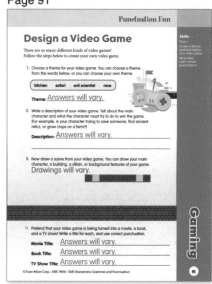

Punctuation Fun

Design a Video Game

There are so many different kinds of video games! Follow the steps below to create your own video game.

1. Choose a theme for your video game. You can choose a theme from the words below, or you can choose your own theme.
   kitchen   safari   evil scientist   race
   Theme: Answers will vary.

2. Write a description of your video game. Tell about the main character and what the character must try to do to win the game. (For example, is your character trying to save someone, find ancient relics, or grow crops on a farm?)
   Description: Answers will vary.

3. Now draw a scene from your video game. You can draw your main character, a building, a villain, or background features of your game.
   Drawings will vary.

4. Pretend that your video game is being turned into a movie, a book, and a TV show! Write a title for each, and use correct punctuation.
   Movie Title: Answers will vary.
   Book Title: Answers will vary.
   TV Show Title: Answers will vary.

Page 92

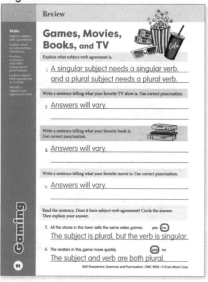

Review

Games, Movies, Books, and TV

Explain what subject-verb agreement is.

1. A singular subject needs a singular verb, and a plural subject needs a plural verb.

Write a sentence telling what your favorite TV show is. Use correct punctuation.

2. Answers will vary.

Write a sentence telling what your favorite book is. Use correct punctuation.

3. Answers will vary.

Write a sentence telling what your favorite movie is. Use correct punctuation.

4. Answers will vary.

Read the sentence. Does it have subject-verb agreement? Circle the answer. Then explain your answer.

5. All the stores in this town sells the same video game. **no**
   The subject is plural, but the verb is singular.

6. The avatars in this game move quickly. **yes**
   The subject and verb are both plural.

Page 93

Story

Read the text.

Astonishing Animals

If you think the animal world is fascinating, then you are not alone. Many people write stories, songs, and poems about the animals they love. The poem "T Is for Tarsier" by Liz Brownlee, for example, kindly describes the tarsier. And "BlobFish Dance Song" is only 30 seconds long, but it still manages to convey the most popular opinion about the blobfish: that it's ugly. In fact, many people find the blobfish interesting enough to write about. The article "Behold the Blobfish" demonstrates this fact.

The tarsier is a tiny primate in Asia, and it has humongous eyes. These cute creatures spend their lives in dense forests, away from humans. The blobfish, on the other hand, is notable because it was voted the "world's ugliest animal" in 2013. Some people say it looks sad because its mouth turns downward, like a frown. The blobfish is from the deep sea and probably looks similar to other fish in its natural environment; however, above water, it appears slimy, like pink jelly.

There is a wide world of beautiful (and ugly) animals to learn about.

Read the rules. Answer the questions.

Grammar An inappropriate shift in verb tense occurs when the verb tense in a sentence or paragraph changes without a reason. We write verbs in the same tense unless there is a reason to change it.

How many blue verbs can you find in the text? **13**

Punctuation We write quotation marks around titles of songs, poems, articles, and short stories.

How many pairs of orange quotation marks can you find in the text? **3**

Page 94

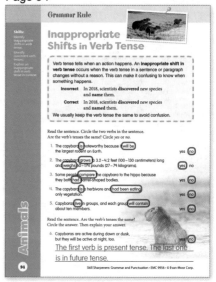

Grammar Rule

Inappropriate Shifts in Verb Tense

Verb tense tells when an action happens. An **inappropriate shift in verb tense** occurs when the verb tense in a sentence or paragraph changes without a reason. This can make it confusing to know when something happens.

Incorrect In 2018, scientists **discovered** new species and **name** them.
Correct In 2018, scientists **discovered** new species and **named** them.

We usually keep the verb tense the same to avoid confusion.

Read the sentence. Circle the two verbs in each sentence. Are the verb's tenses the same? Circle yes or no.

1. The capybara is noteworthy because it will be the largest rodent on Earth. **no**
2. The capybara grows 3.2–4.2 feet (100–130 centimeters) long and weighs 60–174 pounds (27–79 kilograms). **yes**
3. Some people compare the capybara to the hippo because they both had barrel-shaped bodies. **no**
4. The capybara is a herbivore and had been eating only vegetation. **no**
5. Capybaras live in groups, and each group will contain about ten members. **no**

Read the sentence. Are the verb's tenses the same? Circle the answer. Then explain your answer.

6. Capybaras are active during dawn or dusk, but they will be active at night, too. **no**
   The first verb is present tense. The last one is in future tense.

To download a larger version of this answer key, go to: ***www.evan-moor.com/resources***
Enter your email address and this resource code: **EMC9956**

Page 95

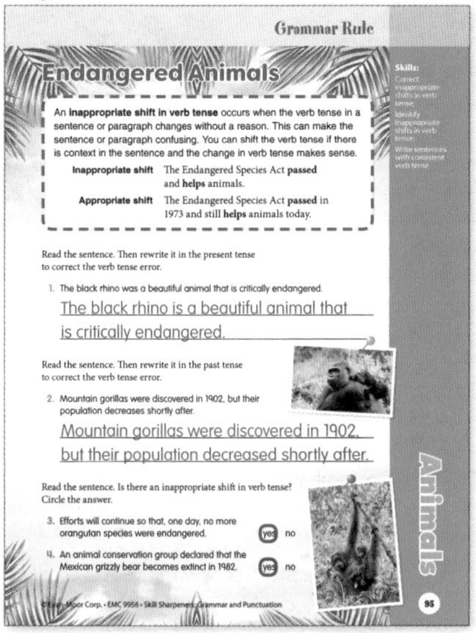

Grammar Rule

Endangered Animals

An **inappropriate shift in verb tense** occurs when the verb tense in a sentence or paragraph changes without a reason. This can make the sentence or paragraph confusing. You can shift the verb tense if there is context in the sentence and the change in verb tense makes sense.

Inappropriate shift The Endangered Species Act **passed** and **helps** animals.

Appropriate shift The Endangered Species Act **passed** in 1973 and still **helps** animals today.

Read the sentence. Then rewrite it in the present tense to correct the verb tense error.

1. The black rhino was a beautiful animal that is critically endangered.
The black rhino is a beautiful animal that is critically endangered.

Read the sentence. Then rewrite it in the past tense to correct the verb tense error.

2. Mountain gorillas were discovered in 1902, but their population decreases shortly after.
Mountain gorillas were discovered in 1902, but their population decreased shortly after.

Read the sentence. Is there an inappropriate shift in verb tense? Circle the answer.

3. Efforts will continue so that, one day, no more orangutan species were endangered. (yes) no
4. An animal conservation group declared that the Mexican grizzly bear becomes extinct in 1982. (yes) no

Skills: Correct inappropriate shifts in verb tense. Identify inappropriate shifts in verb tense. Write sentences with consistent verb tense.

Animals

© Evan-Moor Corp. • EMC 9956 • Skill Sharpeners: Grammar and Punctuation 95

Page 96

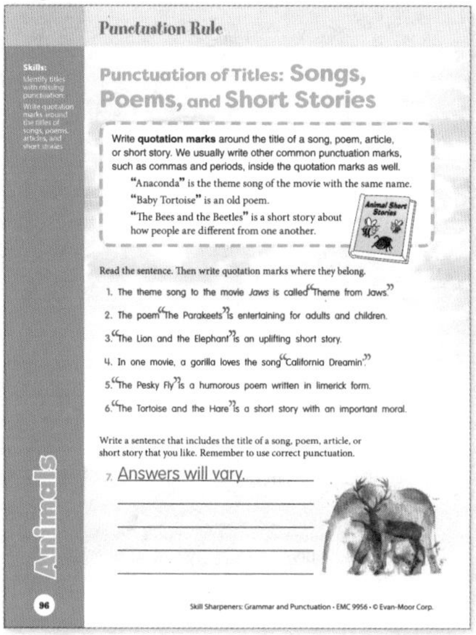

Punctuation Rule

Punctuation of Titles: Songs, Poems, and Short Stories

Write **quotation marks** around the title of a song, poem, article, or short story. We usually write other common punctuation marks, such as commas and periods, inside the quotation marks as well.

"Anaconda" is the theme song of the movie with the same name.
"Baby Tortoise" is an old poem.
"The Bees and the Beetles" is a short story about how people are different from one another.

Read the sentence. Then write quotation marks where they belong.

1. The theme song to the movie *Jaws* is called "Theme from Jaws."
2. The poem "The Parakeets" is entertaining for adults and children.
3. "The Lion and the Elephant" is an uplifting short story.
4. In one movie, a gorilla loves the song "California Dreamin'."
5. "The Pesky Fly" is a humorous poem written in limerick form.
6. "The Tortoise and the Hare" is a short story with an important moral.

Write a sentence that includes the title of a song, poem, article, or short story that you like. Remember to use correct punctuation.

7. Answers will vary.

Skills: Identify titles with missing punctuation. Write quotation marks around the titles of songs, poems, articles, and short stories.

Animals

96 Skill Sharpeners: Grammar and Punctuation • EMC 9956 • © Evan-Moor Corp.

Page 97

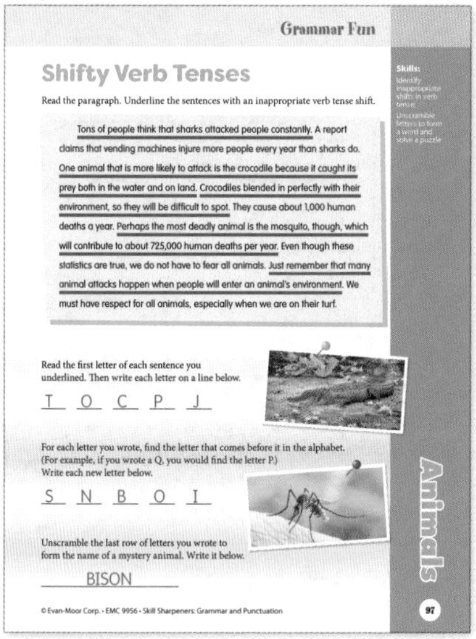

Grammar Fun

Shifty Verb Tenses

Read the paragraph. Underline the sentences with an inappropriate verb tense shift.

Tons of people think that sharks attacked people constantly. A report claims that vending machines injure more people every year than sharks do. One animal that is more likely to attack is the crocodile because it caught its prey both in the water and on land. Crocodiles blended in perfectly with their environment, so they will be difficult to spot. They cause about 1,000 human deaths a year. Perhaps the most deadly animal is the mosquito, though, which will contribute to about 725,000 human deaths per year. Even though these statistics are true, we do not have to fear all animals. Just remember that many animal attacks happen when people will enter an animal's environment. We must have respect for all animals, especially when we are on their turf.

Read the first letter of each sentence you underlined. Then write each letter on a line below.

T O C P J

For each letter you wrote, find the letter that comes before it in the alphabet. (For example, if you wrote a Q, you would find the letter P.) Write each new letter below.

S N B O I

Unscramble the last row of letters you wrote to form the name of a mystery animal. Write it below.

BISON

Skills: Identify inappropriate shifts in verb tense. Unscramble letters to form a word and solve a puzzle.

Animals

© Evan-Moor Corp. • EMC 9956 • Skill Sharpeners: Grammar and Punctuation 97

Page 98

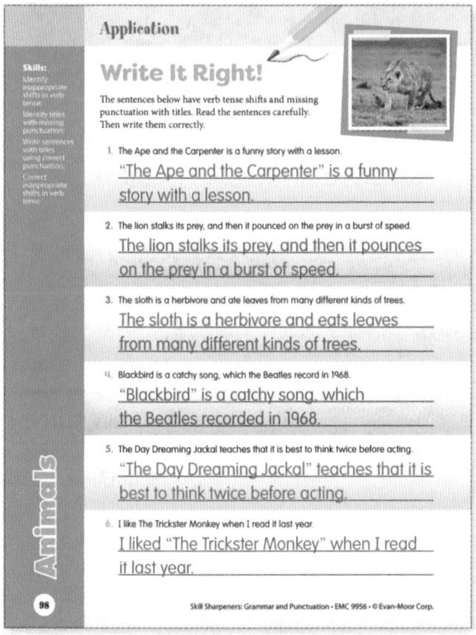

Application

Write It Right!

The sentences below have verb tense shifts and missing punctuation with titles. Read the sentences carefully. Then write them correctly.

1. The Ape and the Carpenter is a funny story with a lesson.
"The Ape and the Carpenter" is a funny story with a lesson.
2. The lion stalks its prey, and then it pounced on the prey in a burst of speed.
The lion stalks its prey, and then it pounces on the prey in a burst of speed.
3. The sloth is a herbivore and ate leaves from many different kinds of trees.
The sloth is a herbivore and eats leaves from many different kinds of trees.
4. Blackbird is a catchy song, which the Beatles record in 1968.
"Blackbird" is a catchy song, which the Beatles recorded in 1968.
5. The Day Dreaming Jackal teaches that it is best to think twice before acting.
"The Day Dreaming Jackal" teaches that it is best to think twice before acting.
6. I like The Trickster Monkey when I read it last year.
I liked "The Trickster Monkey" when I read it last year.

Skills: Identify inappropriate shifts in verb tense. Identify titles with missing punctuation. Write sentences with titles using correct punctuation. Correct inappropriate shifts in verb tense.

Animals

98 Skill Sharpeners: Grammar and Punctuation • EMC 9956 • © Evan-Moor Corp.

Page 99

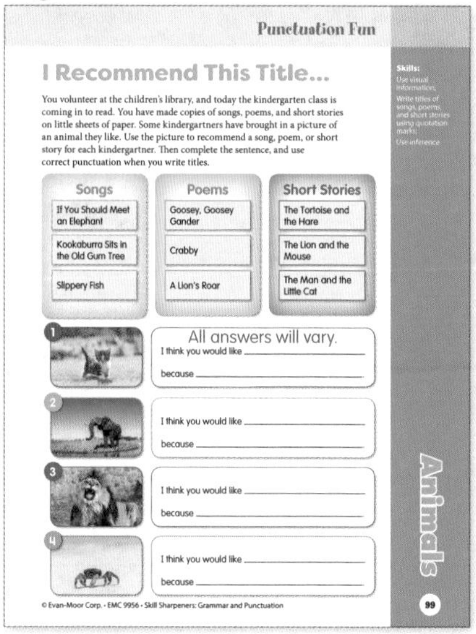

Punctuation Fun

I Recommend This Title...

You volunteer at the children's library, and today the kindergarten class is coming in to read. You have made copies of songs, poems, and short stories on little sheets of paper. Some kindergartners have brought in a picture of an animal they like. Use the picture to recommend a song, poem, or short story for each kindergartner. Then complete the sentence, and use correct punctuation when you write titles.

Songs	Poems	Short Stories
If You Should Meet an Elephant	Goosey, Goosey Gander	The Tortoise and the Hare
Kookaburra Sits in the Old Gum Tree	Crabby	The Lion and the Mouse
Slippery Fish	A Lion's Roar	The Man and the Little Cat

1. All answers will vary. I think you would like ______ because ______
2. I think you would like ______ because ______
3. I think you would like ______ because ______
4. I think you would like ______ because ______

Skills: Use visual information. Write titles of songs, poems, and short stories using quotation marks. Use inference.

Animals

© Evan-Moor Corp. • EMC 9956 • Skill Sharpeners: Grammar and Punctuation 99

Page 100

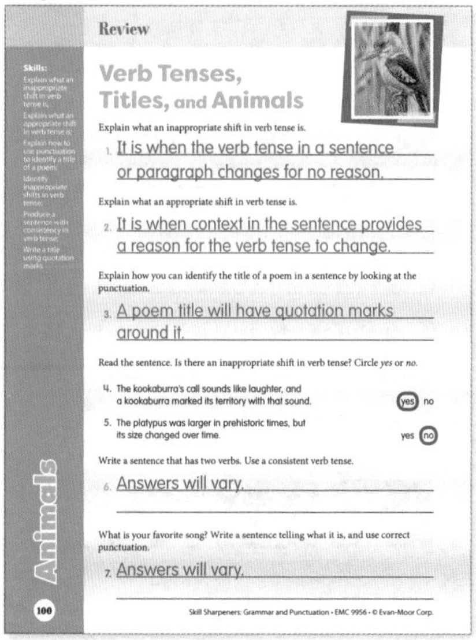

Review

Verb Tenses, Titles, and Animals

Explain what an inappropriate shift in verb tense is.

1. It is when the verb tense in a sentence or paragraph changes for no reason.

Explain what an appropriate shift in verb tense is.

2. It is when context in the sentence provides a reason for the verb tense to change.

Explain how you can identify the title of a poem in a sentence by looking at the punctuation.

3. A poem title will have quotation marks around it.

Read the sentence. Is there an inappropriate shift in verb tense? Circle *yes* or *no*.

4. The kookaburra's call sounds like laughter, and a kookaburra marked its territory with that sound. (yes) no
5. The platypus was larger in prehistoric times, but its size changed over time. yes (no)

Write a sentence that has two verbs. Use a consistent verb tense.

6. Answers will vary.

What is your favorite song? Write a sentence telling what it is, and use correct punctuation.

7. Answers will vary.

Skills: Explain what an inappropriate shift in verb tense is. Explain what an appropriate shift in verb tense is. Explain how to use punctuation to identify a title of a poem. Identify inappropriate shifts in verb tense. Produce a sentence with consistency in verb tense. Write a title using quotation marks.

Animals

100 Skill Sharpeners: Grammar and Punctuation • EMC 9956 • © Evan-Moor Corp.

Page 101

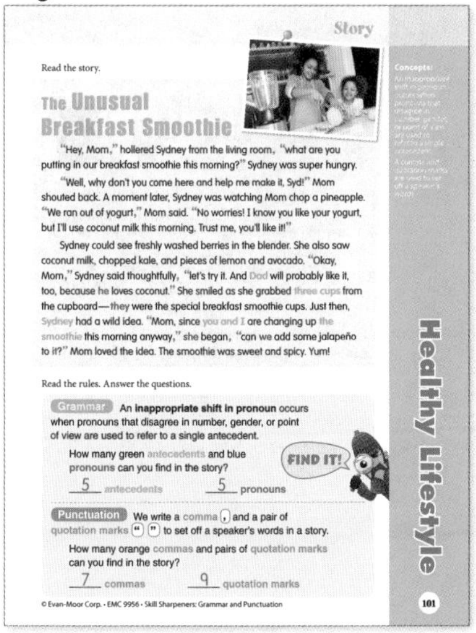

Story

Read the story.

The Unusual Breakfast Smoothie

"Hey, Mom," hollered Sydney from the living room, "what are you putting in our breakfast smoothie this morning?" Sydney was super hungry.

"Well, why don't you come here and help me make it, Syd!" Mom shouted back. A moment later, Sydney was watching Mom chop a pineapple. "We ran out of yogurt," Mom said. "No worries! I know you like your yogurt, but I'll use coconut milk this morning. Trust me, you'll like it!"

Sydney could see freshly washed berries in the blender. She also saw coconut milk, chopped kale, and pieces of lemon and avocado. "Okay, Mom," Sydney said thoughtfully, "let's try it. And Dad will probably like it, too, because he loves coconut." She smiled as she grabbed three cups from the cupboard—they were the special breakfast smoothie cups. Just then, Sydney had a wild idea. "Mom, since you and I are changing up the smoothie this morning anyway," she began, "can we add some jalapeño to it?" Mom loved the idea. The smoothie was sweet and spicy. Yum!

Read the rules. Answer the questions.

Grammar An **inappropriate shift in pronoun** occurs when pronouns that disagree in number, gender, or point of view are used to refer to a single antecedent.

How many green antecedents and blue pronouns can you find in the story?
5 antecedents 5 pronouns

FIND IT!

Punctuation We write a comma (,) and a pair of quotation marks (" ") to set off a speaker's words in a story.

How many orange commas and pairs of quotation marks can you find in the story?
7 commas 9 quotation marks

Concepts: An inappropriate shift in pronoun occurs when pronouns that disagree in number, gender, or point of view are used to refer to a single antecedent. A comma and quotation marks set off a speaker's words in a story.

Healthy Lifestyle

© Evan-Moor Corp. • EMC 9956 • Skill Sharpeners: Grammar and Punctuation 101

Page 102

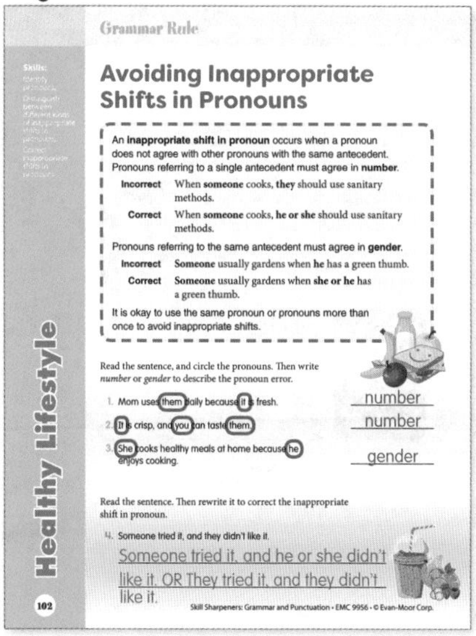

Grammar Rule

Avoiding Inappropriate Shifts in Pronouns

An **inappropriate shift in pronoun** occurs when a pronoun does not agree with other pronouns with the same antecedent. Pronouns referring to a single antecedent must agree in **number**.

Incorrect When **someone** cooks, **they** should use sanitary methods.
Correct When **someone** cooks, **he or she** should use sanitary methods.

Pronouns referring to the same antecedent must agree in **gender**.

Incorrect **Someone** usually gardens when **he** has a green thumb.
Correct **Someone** usually gardens when **she or he** has a green thumb.

It is okay to use the same pronoun or pronouns more than once to avoid inappropriate shifts.

Read the sentence, and circle the pronouns. Then write *number* or *gender* to describe the pronoun error.

1. Mom uses (them) daily because (it) is fresh. number
2. (It) is crisp, and (you) can taste (them). number
3. (She) cooks healthy meals at home because (he) enjoys cooking. gender

Read the sentence. Then rewrite it to correct the inappropriate shift in pronoun.

4. Someone tried it, and they didn't like it.
Someone tried it, and he or she didn't like it. OR They tried it, and they didn't like it.

Skills: Identify pronouns. Distinguish between different types of inappropriate shifts in pronouns. Correct inappropriate shifts in pronouns.

Healthy Lifestyle

102 Skill Sharpeners: Grammar and Punctuation • EMC 9956 • © Evan-Moor Corp.

Page 103

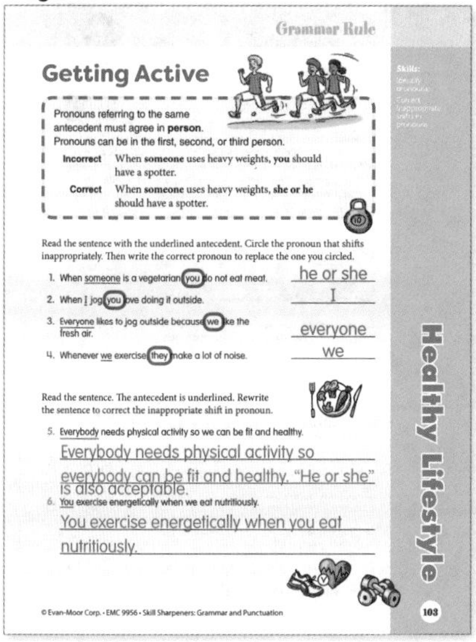

Grammar Rule

Getting Active

Pronouns referring to the same antecedent must agree in **person**. Pronouns can be in the first, second, or third person.

Incorrect When **someone** uses heavy weights, **you** should have a spotter.
Correct When **someone** uses heavy weights, **she or he** should have a spotter.

Read the sentence with the underlined antecedent. Circle the pronoun that shifts inappropriately. Then write the correct pronoun to replace the one you circled.

1. When someone is a vegetarian, (you) do not eat meat. he or she
2. When I jog, (you) love doing it outside. I
3. Everyone likes to jog outside because (we) like the fresh air. everyone
4. Whenever we exercise, (they) make a lot of noise. we

Read the sentence. The antecedent is underlined. Rewrite the sentence to correct the inappropriate shift in pronoun.

5. Everybody needs physical activity so we can be fit and healthy.
Everybody needs physical activity so everybody can be fit and healthy. "He or she" is also acceptable.
6. You exercise energetically when we eat nutritiously.
You exercise energetically when you eat nutritiously.

Skills: Identify and correct inappropriate shifts in pronouns.

Healthy Lifestyle

© Evan-Moor Corp. • EMC 9956 • Skill Sharpeners: Grammar and Punctuation 103

Page 104

Commas and Quotation Marks with Dialogue

Write **commas** and **quotation** marks to set off a quotation in dialogue, or a speaker's exact words in a conversation. Write a comma before or after the exact words. End punctuation and commas usually go inside the quotation marks.

Floyd says, **"**I add nuts and raisins to my oatmeal.**"**
"We need more bananas,**"** Luis tells his mom.

When words interrupt the quotation, write commas and quotation marks to set off only the speaker's exact words.

"If we don't have blueberries,**"** says Nia, **"**we'll use strawberries.**"**

Read the sentence. Then write commas and quotation marks where they belong.

1. **"**Getting plenty of sleep,**"** says Dr. Burl,**"**is important for good health.**"**
2. **"**I feel like I have more energy after I exercise,**"** said Eduardo.
3. **"**I love making salad,**"** said Cole,**"**because I can put any vegetable in it.**"**
4. **"**When I crave a dessert,**"** claims Lupita,**"**I like vanilla yogurt with fruit.**"**
5. Hugh exclaimed,**"**I never thought I'd like cabbage, but I do!**"**

Read the sentence. Then rewrite it with commas and quotation marks where they belong.

6. Amelia says Even though I sprained my ankle, I can still exercise.
Amelia says, "Even though I sprained my ankle, I can still exercise."

Page 105

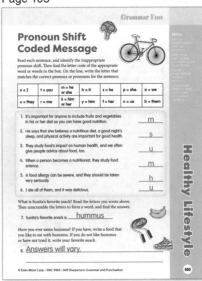

Pronoun Shift Coded Message

Read each sentence, and identify the inappropriate pronoun shift. Then find the letter code of the appropriate word or words in the box. On the line, write the letter that matches the correct pronoun or pronouns for the sentence.

o = I	t = you	m = he or she	h = it	s = he	p = she	a = we
u = they	r = me	k = him or her	y = him	f = her	n = us	b = them

1. It's important for anyone to include fruits and vegetables in his or her diet so you can have good nutrition. — **m**
2. He says that he believes a nutritious diet, a good night's sleep, and physical activity are important for good health. — **s**
3. They study food's impact on human health, and we often give people advice about food, too. — **u**
4. When a person becomes a nutritionist, they study food science. — **m**
5. A food allergy can be severe, and they should be taken very seriously. — **h**
6. I ate all of them, and it was delicious. — **u**

What is Sunita's favorite snack? Read the letters you wrote above. Then unscramble the letters to form a word, and find the answer.

7. Sunita's favorite snack is _hummus_

Have you ever eaten hummus? If you have, write a food that you like to eat with hummus. If you do not like hummus or have not tried it, write your favorite snack.

8. **Answers will vary.**

Page 106

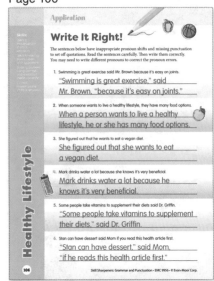

Write It Right!

The sentences below have inappropriate pronoun shifts and missing punctuation to set off quotations. Read the sentences carefully. Then write them correctly. You may need to write different pronouns to correct the pronoun errors.

1. Swimming is great exercise said Mr. Brown because it's easy on joints.
"Swimming is great exercise," said Mr. Brown, "because it's easy on joints."

2. When someone wants to live a healthy lifestyle, they have many food options.
When a person wants to live a healthy lifestyle, he or she has many food options.

3. She figured out that he wants to eat a vegan diet.
She figured out that she wants to eat a vegan diet.

4. Mark drinks water a lot because she knows it's very beneficial.
Mark drinks water a lot because he knows it's very beneficial.

5. Some people take vitamins to supplement their diets said Dr. Griffin.
"Some people take vitamins to supplement their diets," said Dr. Griffin.

6. Stan can have dessert said Mom if you read this health article first.
"Stan can have dessert," said Mom, "if he reads this health article first."

Page 107

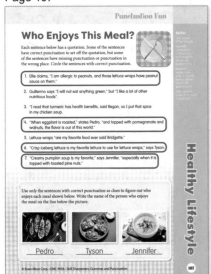

Who Enjoys This Meal?

Each sentence below has a quotation. Some of the sentences have correct punctuation to set off the quotation, but some of the sentences have missing punctuation or punctuation in the wrong place. Circle the sentences with correct punctuation.

1. (Ellie claims, "I am allergic to peanuts, and those lettuce wraps have peanut sauce on them.")
2. Guillermo says "I will not eat anything green," but "I like a lot of other nutritious foods."
3. "I read that turmeric has health benefits, said Regan, so I put that spice in my chicken soup.
4. ("When eggplant is roasted," states Pedro, "and topped with pomegranate and walnuts, the flavor is out of this world.")
5. Lettuce wraps "are my favorite food ever said Bridgette."
6. ("Crisp iceberg lettuce is my favorite lettuce to use for lettuce wraps," says Tyson.)
7. ("Creamy pumpkin soup is my favorite," says Jennifer, "especially when it is topped with toasted pine nuts.")

Use only the sentences with correct punctuation as clues to figure out who enjoys each meal shown below. Write the name of the person who enjoys the meal on the line below the picture.

Pedro   _Tyson_   _Jennifer_

Page 108

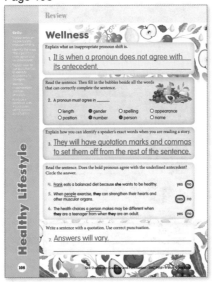

Wellness

Explain what an inappropriate pronoun shift is.

1. It is when a pronoun does not agree with its antecedent.

Read the sentence. Then fill in the bubbles beside all the words that can correctly complete the sentence.

2. A pronoun must agree in ___.
○ length   ● gender   ○ spelling   ○ appearance
○ position   ● number   ● person   ○ name

Explain how you can identify a speaker's exact words when you are reading a story.

3. They will have quotation marks and commas to set them off from the rest of the sentence.

Read the sentence. Does the bold pronoun agree with the underlined antecedent? Circle the answer.

4. Frank eats a balanced diet because **she** wants to be healthy.   yes (no)
5. When people exercise, **they** can strengthen their hearts and other muscular organs.   (yes) no
6. The health choices a person makes may be different when **they** are a teenager from when **they** are an adult.   yes (no)

Write a sentence with a quotation. Use correct punctuation.

7. **Answers will vary.**

Page 109

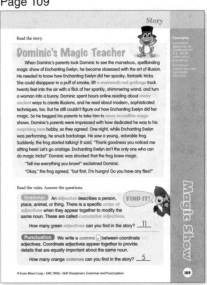

Read the story.

Dominic's Magic Teacher

When Dominic's parents took Dominic to see the marvelous, spellbinding magic show of Enchanting Evelyn, he became obsessed with the art of illusion. He needed to know how Enchanting Evelyn did her spooky, fantastic tricks. She could disappear in a puff of smoke, lift a mammoth red garbage truck twenty feet into the air with a flick of her sparkly, shimmering wand, and turn a woman into a bunny. Dominic spent hours online reading about many ancient ways to create illusions, and he read about modern, sophisticated techniques, too. But he still couldn't figure out how Enchanting Evelyn did her magic. So he begged his parents to take him to more incredible magic shows. Dominic's parents were impressed with how dedicated he was to his surprising new hobby, so they agreed. One night, while Enchanting Evelyn was performing, he snuck backstage. He saw a young, adorable frog. Suddenly, the frog started talking! It said, "Thank goodness you noticed me sitting here! Let's go onstage. Enchanting Evelyn isn't the only one who can do magic tricks!" Dominic was shocked that the frog knew magic.

"Tell me everything you know!" exclaimed Dominic.

"Okay," the frog agreed, "but first, I'm hungry! Do you have any flies?"

Read the rules. Answer the questions.

Grammar An adjective describes a person, place, animal, or thing. There is a specific order of adjectives when they appear together to modify the same noun. These are called cumulative adjectives.   **FIND IT!**

How many green adjectives can you find in the story? _11_

Punctuation We write a comma (,) between coordinate adjectives. Coordinate adjectives appear together to provide details that are equally important about the same noun.

How many orange commas can you find in the story? _5_

Page 110

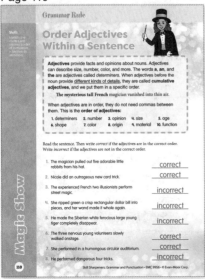

Order Adjectives Within a Sentence

Adjectives provide facts and opinions about nouns. Adjectives can describe size, number, color, and more. The words **a, an,** and **the** are adjectives called **determiners**. When adjectives before the noun provide **different kinds of details**, they are called **cumulative adjectives**, and we put them in a specific order.

The mysterious tall French magician vanished into thin air.

When adjectives are in order, they do not need commas between them. This is the **order of adjectives**:

1. determiners 2. number 3. opinion 4. size 5. age
6. shape 7. color 8. origin 9. material 10. function

Read the sentence. Then write *correct* if the adjectives are in the correct order. Write *incorrect* if the adjectives are not in the correct order.

1. The magician pulled out five adorable little rabbits from his hat. — _correct_
2. Nicole did an outrageous new card trick. — _correct_
3. The experienced French two illusionists perform street magic. — _incorrect_
4. She ripped green a crisp rectangular dollar bill into pieces, and her wand made it whole again. — _incorrect_
5. He made the Siberian white ferocious large young tiger completely disappear. — _incorrect_
6. The three nervous young volunteers slowly walked onstage. — _correct_
7. She performed in a humongous circular auditorium. — _correct_
8. He performed dangerous four tricks. — _incorrect_

Page 111

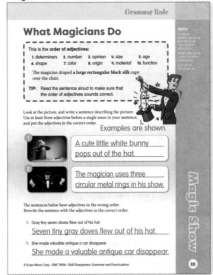

What Magicians Do

This is the **order of adjectives**:
1. determiners 2. number 3. opinion 4. size 5. age
6. shape 7. color 8. origin 9. material 10. function

The magician draped a **large rectangular black silk** cape over the chair.

TIP: Read the sentence aloud to make sure that the order of adjectives sounds correct.

Look at the picture, and write a sentence describing the picture. Use at least three adjectives before a single noun in your sentence, and put the adjectives in the correct order.

Examples are shown.

1. A cute little white bunny pops out of the hat.
2. The magician uses three circular metal rings in his show.

The sentences below have adjectives in the wrong order. Rewrite the sentence so the adjectives are in the correct order.

3. Gray tiny seven doves flew out of his hat.
Seven tiny gray doves flew out of his hat.

4. She made valuable antique a car disappear.
She made a valuable antique car disappear.

Page 112

Commas with Coordinate Adjectives

Write a **comma** between coordinate adjectives. When adjectives before a noun provide **similar kinds of details** or are equal in importance, the adjectives are coordinate.

The wand released a **sweet, fragrant** bouquet of lilies into the air.

The adjectives "sweet" and "fragrant" are coordinate because they both provide a sensory detail about the smell of the noun *bouquet*.

TIP: Switch the positions of the adjectives. If the sentence still sounds correct, then write a comma between the adjectives.

Read the sentence. Then write a comma to separate the coordinate adjectives.

1. The Great Majikeenee was a clumsy, careless magician.
2. His flimsy, weak props often fell apart onstage.
3. When he tried to guess someone's secret, hidden card, he always got it wrong!
4. Once, he meant to release a rabbit, but he released a frightening, dangerous snake instead.
5. His devoted, loyal assistant became injured during a show.
6. His unhappy, disappointed audience always left feeling unimpressed.

Write a sentence with coordinate adjectives. Use correct punctuation.

7. **Answers will vary.**

Page 113

Magic Bubbles Example is shown.

Read the words in the bubbles. Follow the bubbles that form a sentence with adjectives in the correct order. Color each circle that you pass through from **Start** to **End**.

Magic Show

Page 114

Write It Right!

The sentences below have adjectives in the wrong order and are missing commas between coordinate adjectives. Read the sentences carefully. Then write them correctly.

1. The whimsical bizarre magician swooped over the astonished audience.
   The whimsical, bizarre magician swooped over the astonished audience.

2. The oval wooden old large stage was not strong enough to hold all the props.
   The large old oval wooden stage was not strong enough to hold all the props.

3. The magician performed with a blazing sizzling light display on the stage.
   The magician performed with a blazing, sizzling light display on the stage.

4. Gregorio learned magic from outstanding veteran an European illusionist.
   Gregorio learned magic from an outstanding veteran European illusionist.

5. Melissa began doing simple manageable card tricks when she was a child.
   Melissa began doing simple, manageable card tricks when she was a child.

6. Vernon the Talented is a famous brilliant magician who does difficult many illusions.
   Vernon the Talented is a famous, brilliant magician who does many difficult illusions.

Magic Show

Page 115

Is It Really Magic?

Each picture below is an optical illusion. Look at the picture. Then describe what you see in the picture or why you think this picture is unusual.
Examples are shown.

1. You can see the profile, or side view, of the man's face. You can see the man's face from the front, too.

2. It looks like the picture is moving.

Write a sentence about picture number 1 above. Use coordinate adjectives in your sentence, and use correct punctuation.

3. Answers will vary.

Write a sentence about picture number 2 above. Use coordinate adjectives in your sentence, and use correct punctuation.

4. Answers will vary.

Magic Show

Page 116

Magic Show!

Explain what coordinate adjectives are.

1. They are adjectives that appear together and provide similar kinds of details.

Explain why you may want to read a sentence aloud when it has multiple adjectives together.

2. Reading aloud can help you hear whether the order of adjectives sounds correct.

Read the sentence. Then write a comma to separate the coordinate adjectives.

3. With a wave of the wand, the nervous, shaken volunteer disappeared from the stage.

4. When the magician's unsuccessful, failed trick was over, the audience groaned.

5. I have never seen such a daring, risky performance before.

Read the sentence. If the adjectives are in the correct order, write *correct* on the line. If the adjectives are not in the correct order, rewrite the sentence with the adjectives in the correct order.

6. The metal creepy enormous gray rectangular cage floated above the stage.
   The creepy enormous rectangular gray metal cage floated above the stage.

7. The cheerful retired German magician enjoys watching other magicians perform.
   correct

Magic Show

Page 117

Read the text.

The Amazing World of Science

Some facts are so surprising that they seem more like fiction. Did you know that bees could count, for example? Researchers in Australia have trained bees to count, but the bees could count only to four. Want more startling facts? Here are three. And unless you have saliva in your mouth, you cannot taste the flavor of food. Interestingly, people have known for centuries that hot water can freeze more quickly than cold water; scientists are still not completely certain why it happens, though. How do we know all these astonishing facts? Science is the reason! Centuries of research, experimentation, and observation have helped humans develop technology, build structures, make medicine, and gain information about Earth and outer space. There are different science domains. Physical science is the study of natural objects and forces. Life science is the study of living things, and Earth science focuses mainly on the study of Earth and its atmosphere. We are fortunate; we all benefit from the work of scientists.

Read the rules. Answer the questions.

Grammar A text with varied sentence patterns has different kinds of sentences with different lengths, subjects, and word choices.

How many purple sentences with varied sentence patterns can you find in the text? **5**

Punctuation These are some of the ways to correct a run-on sentence. You can write a period and capital letter to make two sentences. Or you can write a semicolon to separate the two independent clauses. A third way is to write a comma and coordinating conjunction to make a compound sentence. FIND IT!

How many orange corrections for run-on sentences can you find in the text? **4**

Science

Page 118

Grammar Rule

Varied Sentence Patterns

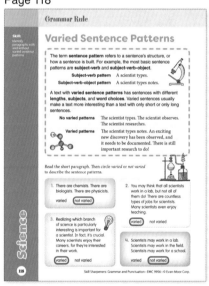

The term **sentence pattern** refers to a sentence's structure, or how a sentence is built. For example, the most basic sentence patterns are **subject-verb** and **subject-verb-object**.

Subject-verb pattern A scientist types.
Subject-verb-object pattern A scientist types notes.

A text with **varied sentence patterns** has sentences with different **lengths**, **subjects**, and **word choices**. Varied sentences usually make a text more interesting than a text with only short or only long sentences.

No varied patterns The scientist types. The scientist observes. The scientist researches.

Varied patterns The scientist types notes. An exciting new discovery has been observed, and it needs to be documented. There is still important research to do!

Read the short paragraph. Then circle *varied* or *not varied* to describe the sentence patterns.

1. There are chemists. There are biologists. There are physicists. varied **not varied**

2. You may think that all scientists work in a lab, but not all of them do! There are countless types of jobs for scientists. Many scientists even enjoy teaching. **varied** not varied

3. Realizing which branch of science is particularly interesting to a scientist is important for a scientist. In fact, it's crucial. Many scientists enjoy their careers, for they're interested in their work. **varied** not varied

4. Scientists may work in a lab. Scientists may work in the field. Scientists may work for a school. varied **not varied**

Science

Page 119

Grammar Rule

Scientists

You can **vary sentence patterns** by using different kinds of sentences. These are some of the kinds of sentences you can use:

Simple Some scientists study sleep.
Compound Scientists may work in medicine, or they may work with robots.
Complex Before they found salts on Mars, scientists didn't know Mars had ever had water on it.
Compound-complex When they froze and then unfroze worms, scientists discovered that the worms kept their memories, and this discovery was surprising.
Interrogative, or a question Does Mars have glaciers?

Read the sentences. Then rewrite them as one compound sentence. Use a comma and the coordinating conjunction **and**.

1. Some scientists study insects. Some scientists study fish.
   Some scientists study insects, and some scientists study fish.

Read the sentences. Then rewrite them as one simple sentence.

2. A scientist may study earthquakes. A scientist may study the weather.
   A scientist may study earthquakes or the weather.

3. Scientists help us make medicine. Scientists help us preserve food.
   Scientists help us make medicine and preserve food.

Science

Page 120

Punctuation Rule

Punctuation to Correct Run-on Sentences

A **run-on sentence** has two or more sentences that are joined together without correct punctuation or a conjunction. Below are some of the ways to correct the following run-on sentence:

Sea horses don't have stomachs they eat constantly.

Use a **period** and a **capital letter** to split the sentence into two.
Sea horses don't have stomachs. They eat constantly.

Use a **semicolon** to separate the independent clauses.
Sea horses don't have stomachs; they eat constantly.

Use a **comma** and a **coordinating conjunction** to make a compound sentence.
Sea horses don't have stomachs, so they eat constantly.

Read the sentence. Is it a run-on? Circle the answer.

1. Camels do not store water in their humps. yes **no**

2. Flamingos are pink their diet of shrimp and algae makes them that color. **yes** no

3. Toucans can curl into a ball they do this when they sleep. **yes** no

4. The smallest bones in the human body are in our ears. yes **no**

Read the sentence. Then write a semicolon to correct the run-on sentence.

5. Each human has a unique smell; it is as unique as a fingerprint.

6. You have no sense of smell when you sleep; odors cannot disrupt sleep.

Science

Page 121

Grammar Fun

Lab Experiments

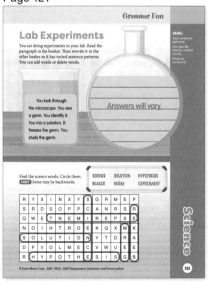

You are doing experiments in your lab. Read the paragraph in the beaker. Then rewrite it in the other beaker so it has varied sentence patterns. You can add words or delete words.

You look through the microscope. You see a germ. You identify it. You mix a solution. It freezes the germ. You study the germ.

Answers will vary.

Find the science words. Circle them.
HINT Some may be backwards.

SCIENCE SOLUTION HYPOTHESIS
BEAKER GERM EXPERIMENT

R	Y	X	I	N	X	Y	S	G	R	M	E	P
S	R	D	S	O	P	P	C	A	N	R	S	R
Q	W	E	T	N	E	M	I	R	E	P	X	E
N	O	I	H	T	R	O	E	K	Q	X	M	K
S	O	L	U	T	I	O	N	Y	T	D	R	A
D	F	V	O	L	M	E	C	V	W	U	E	E
R	H	Y	P	O	T	H	E	S	I	S	E	B

Science

Page 122

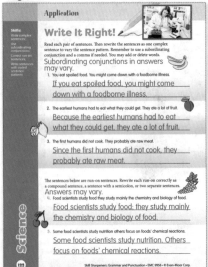

Page 123

Page 124